FUNNY BUSINESS
in 90 MINUTES

For a complete list of Management Books 2000 titles,
visit our website at **www.mb2000.com**

FUNNY BUSINESS in 90 Minutes

Annie Roy-Barker

2000

Dedicated to the memory of my father
My teacher, my inspiration, my dearest friend

This one's for you, Dad

Copyright © Annie Roy-Barker 2006

All rights reserved. No part of this publication may be reproduced, stored in a retrieval system, or transmitted in any form or by any means, electronic, mechanical, photocopying, recording, or otherwise without the prior permission of the publishers.

First published in 2006 by Management Books 2000 Ltd
Forge House, Limes Road
Kemble, Cirencester
Gloucestershire, GL7 6AD, UK
Tel: 0044 (0) 1285 771441
Fax: 0044 (0) 1285 771055
E-mail: info@mb2000.com
Web: www.mb2000.com

Printed and bound in Great Britain by 4edge Ltd of Hockley, Essex – www.4edge.co.uk

This book is sold subject to the condition that it shall not, by way of trade or otherwise, be lent, resold, hired out, or otherwise circulated without the publisher's prior consent in any form of binding or cover other than that in which it is published and without a similar condition including this condition being imposed upon the subsequent purchaser.

British Library Cataloguing in Publication Data is available
ISBN 1-85252-529-0
ISBN13 978-185252-529-2

Contents

	About the Author	7
1	Not an Introduction	9
2	The Benefits of Laughter	19
3	You Cannot Be Serious	31
4	Ban the Boring	39
5	It's Jester Thought	51
6	A Happenstance a Day Keeps the Doctor Away	59
7	Doin' It Your Way	75
8	Humour Aerobics	81
9	Jingle Jangle to the Bank	85

*'Enjoy what you do
and
you will never work a day in your life.'*

Darrell Blake
Managing Director
Blushes Hairdressing Salon, Cheltenham and Gloucester

About the Author

Annie Roy-Barker brings fun and laughter into your business and personal life. She is a popular and accomplished raconteur, whose after-dinner speeches offer you a rare blend of message, motivation and mirth, modelling the speaking style of the future - *entrainment* - the perfect mix of education and entertainment.

Annie started her comedy career working in theatre and cabaret. After making a cynical remark to a customer, which got her fired, she decided to take her humour where it would be better appreciated - and it was, in the corporate conference circuit. For the past 15 years, audiences across the country have appreciated Annie as a unique speaker and performer with a deep knowledge of human communication, relationships and real world skills.

With her infectious passion for life and people, Annie has an adept ability to turn personal experiences into humorous presentations. Her satirical observations on business, motivation and the absurdities of life will do more than elicit your laughter - they will inspire you both personally and professionally.

Annie will raise the roof for you - and your bottom line!

'Worthy of the West End stage! You totally captivated your audience with a riotous blend of anecdotes and up-beat humour, whilst delivering a serious message.'
Ron Aldridge, Actor,
Comedy Writer and Theatre Director

Visit **www.annieroy-barker.com** and sign up to receive Annie's weekly business quips

1

Not an Introduction

'I never did a day's work in my life; it was all fun.'
Thomas Edison

Most books begin with an introduction. This one begins at the beginning and finishes at the end.

In the middle, Annie Roy-Barker (she's the gal who wrote this stuff) offers you a light-hearted approach to serious business.

Funny Business highlights the important role that humour plays in today's business world. It stresses the necessity for enlivening the workplace and making work fun and enjoyable, so that you approach it eagerly, like a passionate hobby.

Funny Business demonstrates how to use humour to increase personal and professional effectiveness, so that people warm to you and are more willing to listen, learn and co-operate with you.

Funny Business has been written with good humour and nothing within its pages is meant to denigrate or upset anyone. If an unintentional blunder offends you, let me get my apology out of the way right now – abjectly, sincerely and unreservedly.

In keeping with my life's tradition of denying any responsibility for my actions, I hold the following people totally accountable for the invasion of this book into your life.

My Mother	Ambiguous insanity and lumpy gravy
My Father	Unconventional rationale and fun times
My Grandfather	Vague rebelliousness and deep morals
Uncle Bill	Absurd uncertainty and very hot curry

James Alexander	Fearless fortitude and paranormal belief
Adrian Smith	Obscure opportunity and ridiculous thinking
John Procter	Unwavering uncertainty and support
Johnnie Cook	Eclectic eccentricity and effervescent banter
Adrian Smith – again	Computer resuscitator extraordinaire

****

I hope you enjoy the Chuckles sections that have been smuggled in here and there.

These scatterings of booty contain funny quotations, humorous stories and snippets of fun that I've collected along life's way. Wherever possible, I've given credit to its originator. Sometimes, however, I have been unable to trace the creators of these little gems of fun. Therefore, I ask all those concerned to accept my acknowledgement and grateful thanks for your good humour and much valued contributions to this book.

Funny Business is an extremely rare publication

This book is extremely sensitive and its feelings run deep, which render it susceptible to claustrophobia. Please, therefore, do not read this book once and relegate it to the bookshelf. Such conditions could cause its pages to shake with fear, rapidly progressing to violent paroxysms of terror.

To preserve the jovial health of both you and this book, please read and enjoy these pages, over and over again. Make regular pit-stops for coffee, iced buns or phone calls to the RSPCFB (Royal Society For The Prevention Of Cruelty To Funny Business) and anything else that helps to re-fill your humour battery, re-charge your laughter engine and pep up your business funny bone.

Funny Business is not just for Christmas – it's for life

You can choose to read this quirky, impish book in your own time or in Greenwich Meantime. Maybe you're lucky and both of these times

Not an Introduction

coincide for you.

Me? Co-ordination never has been one of my strengths, to which each and every one of my long suffering (now grey-haired) piano teachers will testify.

Whatever ... just take some time out and relax, tune into that nimble part of your mind, and enjoy reading *Funny Business* in the most appropriate manner – and place – for you.

Maybe you'll choose the conventional way, sitting down; or do you prefer to read whilst standing on your head in a crowded train? (I always vote for this way. It ensures that the title is visible to fellow passengers).

You might even decide to read *Funny Business* back to front, upside down, skip around it and then end up in the middle. And it's worth remembering the enormous advantages of perusing these pages during a company bored meeting, thereby preventing your slightly suicidal feelings exploding under 'any other business.'

Oh, keep the corporate peace, folk. Remember, you have bills to pay and a life to live – and *Funny Business* aims to show you how to enjoy doing just that! A whole lot more!

Let these pages make you chuckle and, whilst you're busy doing that, be aware that you'll be absorbing ways to see, hear and think about 'all things business' in a more humorous way.

It's a known fact that we all learn a whole lot better, and a whole lot more, when we're enjoying ourselves, than we do through any amount of serious, formal, text book stuff.

However, I do appreciate that some of you may suffer from withdrawal symptoms through removing all seriousness from life, stone cold turkey; so there are some slightly more 'sedate patches' tucked inside these pages. (These work like 'nicotine patches' except you absorb 'em through the mind instead of the skin).

And, so the analytically orientated and the info seekers amongst you don't feel deprived, I've included a few statistics here and there and also tucked in one or two items of reasonably staid research.

Not my research, I hasten to add. I don't do conventional research, being the come-day-go-day-have-fun-now-day lass that I am.

I *do* the *hands on* stuff. My humorous attitude to life and work is the result of getting right in there, just doing it and having fun.

Because humour is individual to everyone, we all develop our own unique sense of humour.

Design a sense of humour?

Do what ???

Pow! That heartfelt exclamation is loudly reverberating round my middle ear drum like an escaped, uncontrollable, Catherine Wheel on bonfire night

And, well ... readers, I've heard all these comments before ...

You must be joking! What? Make work fun? But work isn't supposed to be fun! No siree, you can't mix business with pleasure! Surely you can't be serious?

Absolutely right, folk – you can't be serious ... if you want to squeeze every last drop of juicy fun from this book. And life!

Be clear however. Although it's possible to read *Funny Business* in ninety minutes, you don't have to brace yourself for an hour and a half of belly aching laughter. (Although that would be an excellent way to lose weight)

Such frivolity could be exhausting, even for the most energetic of readers, and that would be no joke.

Anyhow, this book isn't offering jokes. It's offering a liberal blend of education, humour and entertainment, with the aim of provoking you to read, laugh, learn and think differently – through the very way *Funny Business* is put together.

Funny Business flits between whacky and serious, with important bits everywhere, so that you can't see the join.

Please resist the temptation to analyse anything in this book that you don't understand. Humour is insane logic; so quit any attempt to apply even a gnat's size intellect to it.

Just allow the words on these pages to dawdle and comfortably drift into your humour wedge and you will, subconsciously, be

Not an Introduction

dissecting the way humour can be created, spoken and written.

Humour is a process that's awakened by looking at the same things as everybody else and seeing them differently.

Think Picasso. He never saw things in perspective.

Humour, funniness, call it what you will, is created with exactly the same method that Picasso used to create his unique art – through a change in perception.

Funniness – that certain something

'I want to reach your mind. Where is it currently located?'
Ashleigh Brilliant

What is funniness? That 'certain something' that creates the phenomenon called laughter, causes our faces to crumple, our diaphragms to shudder, our mouths to tremble and emit vibrations that sound like a witch's cackling, while our eyes crinkle, sometimes to the point of shedding tears that stream uncontrollably down vibrating cheeks?

We may have been tickled, (and not just pink) or had a dose of laughing gas put in our Christmas stocking.

Although we usually laugh when we're happy, surprisingly, some people laugh because they're fearful, tense, or embarrassed. Sometimes, we laugh simply because we hear the sound of other people laughing – and that is just so wonderfully contagious!

Or we laugh because we find something funny. Which is where we came in. 'What is funniness?'

Well, now, if I could come up with a definition, I would certainly polish my halo, preen my hair and clean out my goldfish. Because there have been many, including Aristotle and Freud, who have failed to define humour.

Billy Crystal, the actor and comedian, didn't waste his time on the theory of it all. He simply stated that:

'There's no explaining why something is funny. It just is.'

Conscious sense is *not* what humour is all about.

So ... what is it about?

Humour is all about tuning into your own extreme, illogical, crazy way of thinking, misinterpreting and deliberately misunderstanding the obvious. It's putting your own stamp on life's happenings and shaking frivolity out of potentially stressful situations; it's about using fun to keep your head when all around you are losing theirs. (Apologies and thanks to Rudyard Kipling).

Real humour finds courteous comedy in discourteous disaster.
Annie Roy-Barker

Not an Introduction

NB: Stay clear of the temptation to plagiarise humour. Although you may get away with this once or twice, it's ultimately guaranteed, 'fall flat on your face' stuff. Having said this, it's a known fact that all top comedians have a repertoire of ad libs and they extract funny remarks from this memory bank as and when the occasion arises.

Now, my friends, I reckon it's time to tickle those funny bones, polish your chuckleometer, pop the humour pills and get set to enter the humorous world of business with all the verve and vigour that's normally reserved for cleaning the bath.
 Erm ...well ... just a tad more would be mighty useful!

Whilst you're preparing to locate, polish and pop, here are a few lesser-known bits about Annie.

Name:	Annie Roy-Barker
Who???	She wrote this book
Birthday:	December 27
Year:	Every year
Parents:	Mother and Father
Birthplace:	Way outside the box
Current home:	Middle of somewhere
Profession:	Speaker and author
Favourite guy:	Mine, though will ditch him if Neil Sedaka makes me an offer
Enjoy:	Having fun with my two granddaughters. (I know, I know. I just don't look old enough)
Don't understand:	'Men are from Mars. Women are from Venus'
Good at:	Procrastinating. I do it bang on time, every time
Favourite word:	Duh (it's such a scientific word)
Word that best describes me:	Eccentric
Ambition:	To be a seriously over-rated sex symbol
Passionate about:	Creating organisations in which people, humour and profits flourish.

Humour breaks

These are so good for us and it's important to make time for the therapeutic magic that these will bring into your life. I urge you to enjoy them unreservedly throughout each and every day.

Starting right now with these frivolous chuckly bits – like I said, you'll find these scattered throughout this book.

So, folk, get your cheek muscles twitching, those humour buds into spasms and rrrrev up your chuckle zone with these notices that folk have collected on their jollies around the world.

Chuckles

Japanese hotel room: Please to bathe inside the tub.

Men's clothing store: 15 men's wool suits £40 - they won't last an hour.

Advertisement: Men wanted to work in dynamite factory. Must be willing to travel.

Nairobi restaurant: Customers who find our waitresses rude should see the manager.

Moscow hotel room: If this is your first visit to the USSR, you're welcome to it.

Budapest zoo: Do not feed the animals. Food should be given to the guard on duty.

Maine restaurant: Open 7 days a week and at weekends.

Dinner special: Turkey £2.50 : Chicken/beef £2.25 : Children £2

Hotel in Athens: Visitors should complain at the office between 9am & 11am daily.

Moscow hotel, by the side of a Russian Orthodox Monastery: You are welcome to visit the cemetery, where famous Russian and Soviet composers, artists and writers are buried daily except Thursday.

Doctor's office in Rome: Specialist in women and other diseases.

Not an Introduction

Q What makes these well-intentioned statements so funny?
A The incongruous way in which they are written.

Humour is created through the unexpected; by introducing an element of surprise.

Humour is a funny way of being serious.

Charlie Chaplin, the king of early comedy, was once asked:
  'Why do people find humour in a man walking down the street and slipping on a banana peel?'
  Chaplin is reported to have replied, *'That is not funny. What is funny is a guy walking down the street and jumping over a banana peel and landing in an open manhole!'*

Q Why is it funny?
A It's unexpected.

We're conditioned to believe that we will slip on a banana skin. So, if you're watching a film, and the guy steps on a banana skin you expect him to slip. When it doesn't happen – the expected that is – you don't have time to get your head around that before, 'pow' the guy falls down an open manhole.
  It's so simple and yet watching somebody do this kind of stupid thing can make us laugh until we cry.
  Hey, you didn't need me to explain how this rubbish works, did you? You knew it all along. So, I guess writing it down just makes me feel that I'm giving you more value for your money.
  Duh! (there's that scientific word again)

Surprise + Unexpected = Incongruence

'Incongruity is the mainspring of laughter.'
                                    Max Beerbohm

2

The Benefits of Laughter

Extract from *The Daily Mail*, Tuesday April 4th 2006

'It's official. Scientists are now proclaiming the benefits of laughter. It has long been held that laughter is the best medicine; and research shows that even the expectation of something funny is good for our health.

Scientists have found that even the anticipation of watching a comedy is sufficient to raise the levels of feel-good endorphins in our body and also double the level of hormones that help us fight off infection.

Experiments, therefore, are proving that laughter not only lifts our spirits, it also boosts our immune system. And the effects of a good laugh can last for up to a day.

Lead researcher Dr Lee Berk, from Loma Linda University in California, said: "It may sound corny, but we need to get serious about happiness and the lifestyle that produces it. I would suggest that you laugh as often as you can."'

The grapevine

Now, readers, wouldn't it be just wonderful if the pharmaceutical companies could actually produce this highly valued commodity called laughter?

But wait! My scandalous, luscious grapevine informs me that laughter could already be available at your local Deli – wrapped in daffodil yellow, giant-sized hilarity packs and tied with frothy pink garden twine.

P.S. Beware! There are many imitation packs on the market, so do make absolutely certain you buy the authentic stuff, boldly labelled as follows:

> **Powerful Hilarious Laughter**
>
> **For rapid and effective decrease of stress and the eradication of tension.**
>
> **Directions for use: Spread frequently and in generous dollops.**

So, for all you would-be multi-millionaires, 'esses' or 'persons' (jeepers, one has to be so careful about political correctness these days. And all I want to do is be happy!), just bottle some laughter, or pack a loud guffaw into a pill, and the world is your oyster!

Just imagine, a super drug that has the ability to cure everything from minor blues to deep depression, heart disease and stress. It has got to be a winner!

Hey, just hang on a cotton pickin' minute. I digress. The zillion benefits of laughter is nothing new to folk like me who live life to the full on a diet of baked beans, giggles and lettuce which, by the by, must surely be an aphrodisiac. Well ...

... there are an awful lot of rabbits! And these rabbits sure seem to know the powerful force of laughter. Just look at an Easter card. There's usually a rabbit on the front jumping over eggs, with a silly grin on its face, wishing everyone a Happy Easter.

Well, now, it's time for rabbits, you and the entire working world, to grin a whole lot more. Because laughter has been brought out of the closet – it's been legalised. So you can now, openly, have fun at work as well as at weekends, bank holidays and coronations.

Whoopee! You don't have to bury your face in your handkerchief or hide your face in the filing cabinet any more.

The Benefits of Laughter

What a relief! Because, you know, it's our natural instinct to turn to laughter when we want to loosen up, lighten up and settle down. Why else would millions of us – from Las Vegas, Ontario and the south side of Skegness – tune in time and time again to chuckle our way through countless repeats of British sitcoms like Fawlty Towers, Porridge, Blackadder, The Office? For me, (hands high, I admit it), I'm totally hooked on the American series Frasier. I drop everything (hmmmm) to watch this American series, with its exceptional, quick-witted, tongue in cheek humour. For me, Frasier has great big empire-state-building, whacky humour and I think the way the scriptwriters play with words is awesome.

Which leads me very nicely, in a roundabout, illogical sort of way, to newspapers. Take a look at how the inappropriate configuration of words in the following headlines creates humour through incongruence.

Headline Chuckles

Include your children when baking cookies

Steals clock: faces time

Hospitals are sued by 7 foot doctors

'Plane too close to ground' crash probe told

Eye Drops off shelf

Two Soviet ships collide, one dies

Squad helps dog bite victim

Shot off woman's leg helps Nicklaus to 66

Miners refuse to work after death

Stolen painting found by tree

Killer sentenced to die for second time in ten years

Some pieces of Rock Hudson sold at auction

Headlines like these (which were collected by journalists) can, and do, sell newspapers. However inadvertently – or not!

The incorrect formation of words is a powerful trigger for our imagination.

Now, this gets me thinking. Just who was the person (keep those postcards rollin' folk) who decreed, all those yonks of years ago, that words should be placed in a certain format in order to create grammatically correct sentences?

Who was it, I would like to know, that invented nouns, verbs, adjectives, and all those other bits I frequently forget to remember?

Was it (apologies if it's you; I'm only being flippant) the same visually impaired person who created our ancient National Curriculum for schools? The 'academic one' who seemed to believe that reading, writing and arithmetic all began with the letter 'R' and decreed that these very same Rs should be the paving stones for the education of our business gurus of the future?

Surely, now, this very idea is enough to jet propel any dedicated hermit out of his cave and onto his soapbox at Speakers' Corner. From whence Mr Hermit will vehemently proclaim that there is more to business success than an alphabet, a quill pen and an abacus.

Of course, Mr Hermit, having been catapulted into modern society after many years in his dark, damp cave, will come to realise that we now eruditely refer to the alphabet as a computer; a quill pen as a printer; and an abacus as a calculator.

What Mr Hermit will also learn, shivering in his loin cloth and peering over his lectern at an incredulous crowd in Hyde Park, is that today's workforce is far removed from his time as leader of the local woodcutters huddle.

In Mr Hermit's day, the main incentive for doing a job was to earn the money that fuelled the fire that roasted the hog that kept the wolf from the cave. Those days are gone.

Our modern workforce not only seeks, it demands a great deal more than Mr Hermit ever did in his day. In addition to financial remuneration with a parking space; unlimited cups of freshly percolated coffee with sugar in perfectly formed cubes; and a signed declaration that Santa Claus and the Tooth Fairy actually exist, today's workforce wants, nay needs, personal and job satisfaction.

What's more, if folk *don't* get that satisfaction, they quit! Believe me, they do!!

Wow ..... I'm hearing the boss's loud cry right now ... !!

'What? You mean that you don't want to go on the Company trip? To visit Santa Claus in Lapland? With all expenses paid?'

'Fraid so, sir. It's a dead cert. Because, when people don't get their basic needs met, they sure do manage to build up a whole lot of resentment inside – to the point where they can (okay, I know this sounds crazy) actually resent the money they're earning.

We'll come back and take a look at our basic needs a little later.

For now, let's consider what Laurie Puhn, relationship and communication expert, has to say about the number one reason for employees resigning from their jobs.

Laurie states:

FACT:
The #1 reason people quit their jobs is a bad boss or immediate supervisor.

FACT:
At any given time, over 50% of the working population are thinking about leaving their jobs. Those who decide to stay cite an excellent relationship with their boss and the enjoyment of their work as their reasons to stay.

CONCLUSION:
Bosses who appreciate and value their assistants' efforts on a daily basis maintain a lower employee turnover rate and a higher productivity rate than the bosses who don't. Why? Because employees who are appreciated and valued for their work respond by valuing and appreciating their bosses. The result is employees:
    (1) stay at their job longer, and
    (2) work harder because of the recognition they receive from their boss.

Are you a boss? Good or bad?

Take Laurie Puhn's **Boss Evaluation Quiz** and find out.

1. Do you give positive feedback to your assistants on a daily basis?
2. Do you ask your assistants for their opinions and suggestions?
3. Do you clearly define job duties and deadlines so that your assistants know how they fits into the scheme of things?
4. Do you find opportunities to praise your assistants in public?
5. When something goes wrong, do you give your assistants time to explain what happened before you rush to judgement?

If you answered 'yes' to all 5 questions:
You are an excellent boss who is a wonderful role model for your company. You recognise the importance of positive interpersonal relationships in the workplace environment and how those relationships connect to the overall success of your company.

If you answered 'yes' to 3 or 4 questions:
You are a satisfactory boss who should consider making some changes if you want to raise the motivational level of your employees, achieve professional success and retain your current assistants.

If you answered 'yes' to 0 or 2 questions:
You are a bad boss who is alienating your assistants, reducing productivity and promoting employee turnover. You should get help in the area of interpersonal communication skills ... immediately!

You can learn the top 35 communication dos and don'ts by reading Laurie Puhn's best-selling book *'Instant Persuasion: How To Change Your Words To Change Your Life'*.

Which take me back to ...

Basic human needs
It's my belief that these can be put into the following broad categories:

1. People need to feel pride and satisfaction in what they're doing
2. People need to feel pride and satisfaction in themselves
3. People need to feel they have some control over their lives
4. People need to feel that their work is enjoyable.

If these basic needs are not met, your workforce will flounder, wither and perish. When they are met, pat yourself on the back, folk. You are nurturing the Midas touch.

Cultivating and nurturing the Midas touch

So, how do you begin to meet the basic needs of your workforce? How do you cultivate and nurture the Midas touch?

With three things – **leadership**, **teamwork** and **passion**

These three powerful commodities, when used effectively, will create an atmosphere of respect, productivity and enjoyment.

'Impossible!' do I hear you say?

'Our man at the top (and, hey, a fair few in between), is just plain miserable.' Well, let's face it, being miserable is the way some folk have fun; just don't let them kid you into believing the same or behaving the same; because it's important for you, me and all the others, to take full responsibility for our working environment and making interaction with colleagues enjoyable.

This means being a leader.

And here's the enigma. It isn't necessary to be at the top to be a leader. You don't have to be a supervisor, manager, director, or be in any position of authority, to take the lead in generating fun.

No siree! You just get right on and lead by example. You take control and create a fun, working environment – and then ... because you're waving your joyful flag, you'll encourage those less extrovert mortals to join you in the happy parade.

Is this all sounding a bit too fundamental? I know it sounds simple yet, hey, trust me. It does work. You'll be The Pied Piper of Humour – everyone will just follow your lead.

Humour rises like warm air

Really invaluable humour – that magical stuff that cultivates good, solid management, employee and customer relations, and encourages creativity and enhances well-being in a workforce – works on the same principle as warm air. It starts on the 'bottom rung' and rises. And it undoubtedly follows, (members of management take note), that company productivity and profitability will also be raised accordingly.

Provided, members of management, that you play your cards right!

So, please heed this warning well. If folk below stairs sense that you disapprove of their happy days and fun-loving methods of improving their life and your company, then employees will begin to restrict their energetic cheerfulness to happy hour, weekends and the allotment.

And the company will lose out big time!

So, management, I urge you to encourage humour! Nay, enjoy and participate in it. Remember the age old adage 'If you can't beat 'em, join 'em.'

Release your own sense of fun and let it trickle down like stalactites of humour, ready and eager to connect with the stalagmites of humour rising from below. And when these two bouncy forces meet – **POW** – there will be such a wonderful explosion of trust, camaraderie and benefits all round.

And what a fantastic position you're in, then, to instigate lots of ideas for promoting more fun and humour within the organisation. Unless you've already done that, of course.

You have? **WELL DONE**. I'm shouting it from the hilltops.

Please, though, always remember that it's vital for humour to rise like warm air. Unless it starts at a lower level and rises, the company will reap little reward. So, members of management, it's important that you accept, acknowledge and embrace every little bit of workplace humour that trickles up towards you.

Little things mean a lot

A friend of mine, Edward, owns an estate in Shropshire. Although he employs a manager to deal with the day to day running of the business, Edward takes a real interest in all his employees. Needless to say, he has an incredibly low turnover of staff and everyone is dedicated to their job and utterly loyal to my friend.

Every employee's birthday is personally acknowledged by Edward; ladies receive an exquisite arrangement of flowers (in their favourite colours) and men are given a bottle of their preferred tipple.

Couples celebrating a wedding anniversary are booked into a restaurant of their choice and Edward will pick up the bill.

All other occasions that are important to each employee are also acknowledged in an equally appropriate and personal way.

Catch 'em doin' it

Not only does Edward take the trouble to remember and honour his employee's special occasions, he's constantly aware of what is going on around him in the workplace. He never takes anyone's dedication and loyalty for granted, having realised forty years ago that these things have to be earned!

So, Edward doesn't continually rely on his Manager to tell him that Fred, Ethel and the tea boy are all doing a good job, or that one of his suppliers has moved heaven and earth to get a delivery to them in break-neck time (ah, yes, please remind me to come back to suppliers). He gets around and notices what's happening for himself.

Edward's 'Happy Chappy' check list
This caring employer, and successful businessman, sincerely wants every member of his 'working family' to:

- have so much fun at work that they look forward to Mondays
- enjoy doing what they do that they want to do it a whole lot more
- be passionate about their work because passion creates commitment.
- get a buzz from their job, because it stimulates new ideas and solutions
- feel that the only work they have to do is the easy kind.

Suppliers (thank you for reminding me)
Edward gets the very best treatment from everyone, because the fun that he creates is widespread. It bubbles over suppliers, customers and Cuthbert, the estate office's cat – they all give of their best, because Edward is passionate about having fun.

How does he do it? Edward would tell you it's because he likes to play and that it's much more enjoyable when everybody plays. He would say it's that simple – to be in the habit of treating everything you have to do as play. In doing this, you give yourself, and others, permission to create fun and laughter.

'Fun and laughter,' says this highly successful man, *'are things to be taken very seriously. They turn work into play and then all jobs are approached with irresistible enthusiasm.'*

Fun is the terra firma of personal and corporate success. Dismiss it at your peril!

What, then, is the right way of living?
Life must be lived as play.
Plato, Greek Philosopher

The Benefits of Laughter

Here are Edward's secrets for successful leadership

- ✓ Motivation through fun and laughter
- ✓ An environment that encourages, incorporates and supports play
- ✓ Regular employee get-togethers to discuss company plans and strategies for the future.
- ✓ Explain why something needs to be done; don't just issue instructions to do it. In other words, make jobs meaningful and fulfilling
- ✓ Never criticise; this reduces creativity, productivity and success.
- ✓ Praise achievements, no matter how small. If a job is only partially completed, praise that part and offer encouragement to finish the rest.
- ✓ Make people feel good about themselves; boost their confidence and self-esteem.
- ✓ Show genuine concern and lead with sincere care for everyone
- ✓ In addition to verbal encouragement and appreciation, show it in practical ways, i.e. time off, social treats, etc.
- ✓ Make employees feel that you are there for them and not the other way around.

Fun = passion = motivation = dedication = loyalty = increased productivity
= SUCCESS

You catch more flies with honey than you do with vinegar.
Dale Carnegie

3

You Cannot Be Serious

Chronic seriousness is the corporate coffin

Chronic seriousness in today's workplace can only succeed in making the corporate coffin-makers rub their hands with glee. So, don't let them get a look in, folk – send them off to make their living from other pickings.

The amount of terminally serious people wandering around is quite disturbing. You'll easily recognise them by their permanently furrowed brow and frequent bad hair days. You'll also notice that they suffer from a debilitating loss of perspective and, therefore, always take themselves far too seriously.

Or should that be the other way around?

Whatever, these poor souls (who, by the way, run a far greater risk of developing heart problems than their cheerful counterparts) inevitably end up in their GP's surgery, get diagnosed as suffering from stress or depression, pop the tranquillisers, have endless time off work ... covered by an all-embracing sick note ... and, hey, this happens over and over again, with each patient seemingly desperate to get into the Guinness Book of Records for losing the most time and money for their employer.

Duh! Here's that scientific word again.

The best medicine for overcoming terminal seriousness – and preserving good mental health – is laughter. This powerful stress buster soothes your mind like mental floss and whacks out the worry that tends to cling to your brain like a dose of super powered Velcro.

A good dose of laughter allows you to challenge problems with a clear head and a healthier heart.

Laughter, this valuable, infinite resource is readily available and absolutely free.

So use it! Seriousness is a definite No! No! No! It's time to kick it into touch and make a promise to yourself and the world that you, and every member of your workforce, will be encouraged to use humour to live a healthy, sane, balanced life.

Make that promise right now and you're on the way to greater motivation; improved morale and health; better communication; strengthened trust, at all levels, within the company; more efficient customer service; and increased productivity.

> *Incentive* magazine reported that Dawn Morrelli, of Honeywell, proved that fun and productivity do measure up.
>
> Dawn, apparently, is known as the 'calendar girl' within the organisation (not to be confused with the Women's Institute calendar girls; now there's a fun way to do business) because she uses two calendars – one for keeping track of time in the conventional way and the other, for keeping tabs on the number of days saved whenever a project gets finished ahead of time.
>
> Dawn, apparently, uses the days saved to reward employees for their valued input into the company.
>
> She does this by using her fictitious calendar. When a public holiday comes around, Dawn encourages every member of her workforce to celebrate it. Therefore, it's not unusual for Valentine cards to circulate in August; Easter eggs to be enjoyed in September; and New Year's greetings to resound in the height of summer.
>
> In one instance, the number of days saved added up to five months, meaning that Dawn's staff had actually completed enough early deliveries to merit observing two year's worth of holidays and raised Honeywell's on-time delivery rate from 75% to 87% !!

Hey, folk, celebrating every one of your favourite holidays three times a year has just gotta be good, eh?

And there's more to the snowball
What better way to attract top-notch employees, (those high calibre, ultra-efficient folk that don't even think about wagging because they're passionate about their work and it's so much fun) and then ... hold on to these valuable members of your healthy, happy, workforce.

Would that reduce your stress level?

Let's think about stress

It's a little six-letter word that can give you big trouble.

Consider it for a moment. *Hey, stop! That's long enough.* Focus on stress and that's what you'll get. Focus on not getting stressed. And surprise, surprise. You still get stressed; because you'll always get more of what you focus on – whether you're thinking negatively or positively.

So, here's where you must start to find something amusing in every situation. **And make fun and laughter your focus.**

Oh, yes you can. I know you can.

As well as offering *'the quality of being amusing or comic'*, the Oxford Reference Dictionary defines humour as *'a state of mind, mood, inclination.'* Humour, therefore, is all about attitude; it's about taking things less seriously; it's about freely laughing at yourself and situations. It's about thinking and looking at things in a different way.

Remember Picasso? Fun is seeing things from a different perspective.

Now, it's possible you may be thinking that having fun is easier said than done; that it's all very well for me to tell you to see the funny side of things but – oh dear – it doesn't work for you because you don't have a natural wit and ready sense of humour ...

Folk, here's the wonderful, great big empire-state-building, good news.

Anyone can learn to think in a fun kind of way and begin to see things from a humorous point of view. You may not get to be a stand-up comic with an endless, ready supply of jokes on the tip of your tongue but, as I've said before, and I'll just keep right on repeating it, humour is not about telling jokes, being funny, or looking foolish; though you're free to do so, if it helps you sleep better at night!

Fun at work is created by developing skills and creating habits that influence and encourage you to enjoy what you do.

Like, for example, when you receive an annoying email, instead of getting your paddy up, sending your blood pressure through the roof and throwing your monocle at the computer, just say, right out loud *'ha ha, hee hee hee, ho ho'*. And ...

> **Notice how your life brightens -**
> **That Velcro strip of worry lightens -**
> **And your mood just heightens.**

(Okay, I don't expect the Nobel Prize for Literature)

The only way to feel happy is to put yourself there

Hold on to this thought if you still reckon that you can't get your head around this humour stuff. It is possible to learn how to think more humorously, just as you learned how to walk.

When you took your first step and fell flat on your face, did you say: *'I quit. I'm not even going to attempt to walk again. It's too difficult. Walking is impossible?'*

Not on your little Nelly. It never occurred to you that you couldn't do it, so you just kept on trying until, now, you can do it automatically. (Forgive me if you can't.)

As children, we have an incredible, innate ability to achieve things, simply because we can imagine doing them. And it never occurs to us, as children, that 'our dreams' will never turn into reality. So, go back, start again and .....

Learn humour

If at first you don't succeed, remove all evidence of such attempts and turn to the best, and by far the easiest, way to 'learn to think humour'. By mixing with humorous people and reading humorously written books, articles, stories – anything that you can buy, beg or borrow. Doing this will encourage fun thinking to seep into your guffaw-releasing enzymes and allow your own humour to bubble to the surface. It's there inside you. Waiting! Yes, really. Everyone has a sense of humour – it's just that, in some people, it's like a dormant volcano.

And what does a volcano do?

Given the right conditions, it will erupt.

And your sense of humour will erupt in exactly the same way; set the scene and your chuckle zone will bounce into activity.

A guy called Bob encouraged my volcano into action. We worked together and he made every day such incredible fun. He had the ability to laugh his way through anything, make mountains into molehills and always saw the funny side of any corporate catastrophe. Bob reckoned he'd 'caught' his humour from his father. And, (lucky me) I caught it from Bob.

Humour sure is contagious!

When you've caught it strongly enough, and you've developed the ability to laugh at tricky circumstances and difficult problems, then you get to feel a sense of superiority and power over these situations; a positive and hopeful attitude emerges when you're able to laugh at things that would, previously, have troubled you.

Humour provides a totally different perspective on difficult issues. It's also a remarkable mechanism for releasing uncomfortable emotions – and these, if left inside to fester, can create harmful, biochemical changes in the body.

Humour is a veritable lifeline

Anywhere and everywhere, an environment of fun is one that is mentally, emotionally and physically healthy. Provided that, at all times, you adhere to …

The Cardinal Rule

 **Never, never, never, attempt to make fun at other peoples' expense.**

At all times, and in all places, humour should be used with the greatest of respect. Please, don't ever be tempted to use it to put anyone down, disguise sarcasm, or exploit the preferences, beliefs, or weaknesses of anyone.

Apart from ... yourself!

Now, we're talking on a different level here, folk. Because the biggest skill you can have in the humour stakes is the ability to be able to laugh at yourself.

Self-deprecating humour is the finest way to amuse others, so you have my permission to wholeheartedly tear your personal foibles to pieces. After you've told a few self-confessional anecdotes, you'll realise this is a sure fire way to guarantee that the world laughs with you.

Oh, yes! Do remember to keep things clean; don't ever risk offending anyone and, believe me, that's easier to do than watching ice cream melt in the sun.

And whilst we're on the subject, I'd just like to mention that respect is the important precursor to successful humour. Fun will always flourish in an atmosphere of courtesy and consideration.

Consider this for a moment ...

Have you ever overheard a person being sarcastic, even rude to someone, and then attempting to laugh it off by saying, *'Oh I'm only joking, you know I don't mean it?'*

Familiarity, readers, does breed contempt. Please, therefore, remember this – respect and sincerity first, humour second. That way, humour will always embrace respect.

No amount of fun and laughter can make up for a lack of integrity. It is committed people, not authority, that produce results.

So find out what works for your organisation and for your colleagues. Get a feel for what is working and what isn't.

Communication

That old chestnut, communication, is the basis of all good relationships in every walk of life, either personal or in business. And by good, I mean honest. This means saying what you mean and meaning what you say. Obvious? Don't folk always do that? No, they certainly don't.

The sad outcome of vague communication is that people don't know where they stand; they become frustrated and disheartened; and they don't feel valued, trusted or respected.

Given these circumstances, how do you rate the chances of any relationship surviving?

Time for another quick rev of the chuckle zone.

Chuckles from the insurance world

Those of you in the insurance sector may already have giggled with these extracts from insurance claim forms.
For those reading these Chuckles for the first time, they are genuine statements made by claimants as the 'excuse' for their accident:

- The car in front hit the pedestrian, but he got up so I hit him again.
- I collided with a stationary truck coming the other way.
- A pedestrian hit me and went under my car.
- The guy was all over the road. I had to swerve a number of times before I hit him.
- I had been driving for forty years when I fell asleep at the wheel and had an accident.
- To avoid hitting the bumper of the car in front I struck a pedestrian.
- I was sure the old fellow would never make it to the other side of the road when I struck him.
- The pedestrian had no idea which way to run as I ran over him.
- The gentleman behind me struck me on the backside. He then went to rest in a bush with just his rear end showing.
- The accident happened when the right front door of a car came round the corner without giving a signal.
- The pedestrian ran for the pavement, but I got him.
- Coming home, I drove into the wrong house and collided with a tree I don't have.
- A pedestrian hit me and went under my car.
- In an attempt to kill a fly, I drove into a telephone pole.
- An invisible car came out of nowhere, struck my car and vanished.
- I was thrown from the car as it left the road. I was later found in a ditch by some cows.

4

Ban the Boring

Boredom kills fun and creativity. So it must be banished.

The first thing to ban, both in your mind and the workplace, is the ridiculous saying, 'Never mix business with pleasure.'

It never ceases to amaze me how people can actually believe that business and pleasure cannot go hand in hand. What's more, these disbelievers can usually be found loudly and proudly proclaiming their outmoded belief from the top of the anaesthetised chimney on the tranquillised rooftop of their very sedated office, in which they lead a monotonous, sterile life.

Just what is going on in the minds of these folk? Or not? Do they want a down-in-the-mouth organisation that not only beckons the corporate coffin makers, it practically pays their account up front? With travel costs and a hefty tip to boot?

These diehard managers would do well to take heed of business author, Paul Hawken. He defines it well:

> *'We lead by being human. We do not lead by being corporate, by being professional, or by being institutional.'*

Listen well, all ye with feet of clay. The trick to creating and maintaining a happy, successful organisation is to always mix business with pleasure; and to constantly strive to find ways of introducing new life and fun into the workplace.

It's my belief that far too many companies are under the illusion that power is the central force of a smooth running, flourishing organisation.

Duh!

Power, without heart, is like a car without an engine; no amount of cranking can bring it to life and make it work, because its very soul is missing – that vibrant, caring, exciting, part that boosts employee morale, creates job satisfaction and prevents burnout.

Fun, laughter, cheerfulness, and happiness are all vital elements in the creation of teams that are able to enjoy and celebrate success.

Circa 1852

The following notice, dated 1852, was apparently found in the ruins of a London office building. It's worth recalling if you ever feel overworked, under-paid and under-valued.

1. This firm has reduced the hours of work and the clerical staff will now only have to be present between the hours of 6am and 7pm.

2. Clothing must be of sober nature. The clerical staff will not disport themselves in raiment of bright colours, nor will they wear hose unless in good repair.

3. Overshoes and topcoats may not be worn in the office, but neck scarves and headwear may be worn in inclement weather.

4. A stove is provided for the benefit of the clerical staff. Coal and wood must be kept in the locker. It is recommended that each member of the clerical staff brings four pounds of coal each day during the cold weather.

5. No member of the clerical staff may leave the room without permission from the supervisor.

6. No talking is allowed during business hours.

7. The craving for tobacco, wine, or spirits is a human weakness and, as such, is forbidden to all members of the clerical staff.

> 8. Now that the hours of business have been drastically reduced, the partaking of food is allowed between 11.30am and noon, but work will not on any account cease!!!
>
> 9. Members of the clerical staff will provide their own pens. A new sharpener is available on application to the supervisor.
>
> 10. The supervisor will nominate a senior clerk to be responsible for the cleanliness of the main office and the supervisor's private office. All boys and juniors will report to him 40 minutes before prayers and will remain after closing hours for similar work. Brushes, brooms, scrubbers, and soap are provided by the owners.

Maybe Circa 1920

'Humour? In the workplace? You've got to be joking,' said the guy on the end, not realising he'd almost *'made a funny.'*

Getting redder in the face, he fingered his starched collar, adjusted his toupee and, with a twitch of his Hercule Poirot moustache, exclaimed, *'No! No! No! We employ people to work. To make a profit for the company. And that ... is no laughing matter!'*

Definitely Circa now

Gone are the days when our main incentive for doing a job was to earn money. Today's workforce has different values.

These are summed up by John Naisbitt in his best selling book *Reinventing The Corporation,* and this extract gives a good insight into how the workplace has changed over the years.

'In the beginning, the workplace flourished through money and machines, but most businesses today find that their chief assets are information, knowledge and creativity.

Emphasis has shifted from financial resources to human resources.

Since using resources profitably is what management is all about, effective managers must search for, and adopt, whatever methods produce the best results.

Looking at today's successful workplaces, you will see they have in common, teamwork, mutual caring and respect, laughter, and a zest for achieving.'

****

And here's another interesting quote:

'People do work for money – but they work even more for meaning in their lives. In fact, they work to have fun. Companies that ignore this fact are essentially bribing their employees and will pay the price in a lack of loyalty and commitment.'
'Six Dangerous Myths About Pay'
Harvard Business Review
Jeffrey Pfeffer

****

So, where now?

You've come to the very place to read about my 'one size fits all' ... 'tried and tested'... 'blanket cover' ... 'do this and you cannot fail' positive procedure for creating a healthy, happy, successful, fun, working environment.

Oh, dream on!

Regrettably ... I have yet to develop such an invaluable strategy.

So, whilst I frantically work out what I can write about next, I'll give you a few questions to ponder, contemplate, think about, deliberate, mull over, consider, and wonder about – my sanity. And yours, by now!

- Are shoes without soles more efficient than birds without wings?
- How does a cuckoo know it's a cuckoo?
- How would you feel if you were born without parents?
- What colour turns red, squishy jelly green?
- Is the speed of dark faster than the speed of light?
- Do baked beans taste the same upside down?
- Why is there only one monopolies commission?
- How do we know when we've achieved the impossible?

Fast Rewind
To carry on from where I was and, as I said (if I didn't, I meant to) way back, every bit of stuff in this book is written with the intention of creating serious humour in the workplace. There's no hard and fast rule for this; no right or wrong way; no good or bad. It just is.

So I'd like you to stop!

And begin to start recollecting how important it is that humour should rise like warm air – from the bottom level upwards. And also remember the importance of management acknowledging and showing its appreciation of this.

With these thoughts in mind, we'll now take a look at:

Annie's Four Strategies For Fun

Strategy For Fun: 1

✓ The workplace and all them that's in it

Take a long, hard look at your organisation. Go on, nobody's watching. (Actually, I hope they are, you'll gain a lot of Brownie Points).

No, no, no, much deeper than that. Stare if you must. And step right into the heart, the very core of your company and its workforce, and notice what's already going on there; and what makes all the folk within it ..... tick.

Come on now. Conscience rules, OK? Don't be tempted to skip this first and extremely important Fun Rule. There's no way you can build a firm empire, however funny it may seem, on weak footings. Remember the story about the three little pigs? Now, there's a serious message that's lost on most children. (Go on, borrow it from some unsuspecting little 'un.)

Human beings think systematically and not randomly; therefore, approach this important Fun Rule in a systematic manner and not running around like a rabid dog chasing a headless chicken.

Folk are different

We're all different. (You bought this book to be told that?) So, the way we like to receive recognition for what we do, whether they are acts of bravery, repairing the photocopier or making the tea, is also different.

First, you need to turn yourself into a Miss Marple, or a Sherlock Holmes, and study the needs of individual members of staff in order to find out their preferences and reactions. What makes them tick? What circumstances bring out the best in them? What is it that you do that makes them respond more positively to you? etc etc.

Also, you need to find out what members of staff do in their leisure time. Are they family orientated? What are their hobbies and interests? How do they find fun?

Go on. Have an impromptu chat with them. It'll make them feel noticed and respected; and they'll soooo enjoy that feeling.

Making a sincere effort to care about your workforce, as individuals and not just numbers on a payroll, is going to reap great rewards for you.

When you've done your homework, now's the time to consider how you can best match their style of fun when they're not at work, at work. (If you get my drift). In other words, how you reward them.

Clearly, the better you get to know your workforce as individuals, the more successful you will be in creating appropriate fun rewards for their personal achievements.

Strategy For Fun: 2

✓ Do, do and do more fun

'Don't do as I do, do as I say.'

Banish this attitude from the depths of your 'might just get away with it' mind with a swish of your swashbuckling thought eraser.

From now on it's top to bottom fun

Think fun : organise fun : promote fun : action fun

Enjoy the brilliance of leading through fun and laughter. Be the very model of serious corporate lunacy and watch how commitment, loyalty, well-being, camaraderie, and production increase like sea, sand and sun on a Caribbean island.

Employees will follow your lead. So, always **do, do and do more fun.**

Lead with gloom and you'll get gloom.

Lead with fun and you'll get fun

Strategy For Fun: 3

✓ Giving is receiving

Now, folk, I'd like you to read the following paragraph carefully and answer the couple of questions at the end. Your answers hold a vital clue as to how you handle people – and life. Here comes the paragraph:

FACT:
Whenever we give, we receive. Not always – ok seldom – do we receive like for like (well, hey, you might as well just keep that box of choccies). It's that, when you give on the material level, you receive a gift on the emotional level.

Q Do you consider that the emotional gift you receive is a good one?
Q How does that gift make you feel?

Now, your answers to both these questions indicate your depth of commitment, both to your personal well-being, and the well-being of every member of your organisation. Because ... when you do something for the benefit of your colleagues and members of your workforce, you should be doing it as much for your benefit as for theirs.

> 'Giving connects two people, the giver and the receiver, and this connection gives birth to a new sense of belonging'
> Deepak Chopra

Creating fun for others, therefore, is obviously a two-way process. You, also, get to enjoy yourself. And you strengthen rapport within your team. And you strengthen the sense of community. And you create a deeper, personal connection with each member of your workforce

To be both a successful and a fulfilled leader, it's absolutely essential that you 'connect' with your employees. Success, without fulfilment, equals an isolated, discontented leader. And that's a very forlorn feeling to face every day.

Strategy For Fun: 4

✓ Slow down Greenwich

If you're anything lie me, this strategy will have the ability to scrabble your mind and send you screaming down the road, shedding your clothes, ambitions and eyelashes along the way.

There is, however, limited time for hiding your embarrassed self in a ditch before stupidity sets in so, as soon as there's a lull in the traffic.

Get back here ... and listen well ...

Be Patient! You can't change a serious corporate culture into a playful group overnight. So, don't even attempt it!

This process of change will need a lot of careful thought and planning in order to ensure that it has an effective, permanent outcome. Take your time, my friends, and allow yourself to savour the gradual process of achievement like a glass of vintage wine. (Now wasn't that a serene passage?)

Begin with a few small events (don't overdo it now, keep it simple) that send unmistakable messages to your workforce that you realise it's time to lighten up the whole caboodle; that your company has come right into this century's way of thinking; and you're even contemplating a 'pets at work' scheme.

Well, you might be!

I mean, I don't know what you're considering, do I? For all I know, you might be at the point of converting your staff restaurant into a refuge for lost homing pigeons.

As an aside, there's a website called **dogster.com** and, according to a survey it carried out, 49% of respondents said they'd switch jobs if they could take their dogs to work; 32% said they'd take a pay cut if they could bring Rover, Fido, or whatsitsname along; and – here comes the big one! – 66% said they'd work longer hours if doggy could join them at the office.

Yes, I know (don't bother with the emails) these percentages total 147%. Just a bit of overlap.

I've always thought it would be fun to have a dog, called Guess. Imagine the scenario:

'What's your dog's name?'
'Guess.'
'Rover? Patch? Blacky?
'No, Guess.'
'Clarissa? Oswald? Cuthbert?'

And you just shake your head ... and let folk lie awake at night, pondering this one; they'll make endless lists and e-mail them to you at 2am; and then cross you off their Christmas card list when 'sense of humour failure' kicks in with a vengeance.

Here's a good place to quote that all time great, Albert Einstein.

> *'Only two things are infinite, the universe and human stupidity, and I'm not sure about the former'*

Talking about infinity ...

Relegate the word *'meeting'* to the veritable scrap heap of infinity and find a more exciting and worthwhile title. Do find (nay, even invent) an imaginative name that entices everyone to do a soft shoe shuffle, witty report in hand, to attend your oh so stimulating jamborees. Now, there's a descriptive moniker. (Look it up. I didn't know what it meant either, until it jumped out of the thesaurus).

Now, you need to pep up your agenda. And just watch all those hitherto jaded faces turn into smiling rays of eager creativity and optimism, as their eyes alight on that pepped up piece of paper.

What did I say? Pepped up agenda!

Sure. Get set to ditch that boring sheet of paper and all its repetitive lines. They're so carved in stone that you could recite them in your sleep.

It's 'make your agenda snazzy' time folk. Oh, so snazzy that it creates relentless, unrestrained action from all fellow 'jamborians.'

Give your agenda a theme. For example, you could use book or song titles as headings for each item.

Buy a joke book, or get some jolly one-liners off the web, and scatter them in the margins of your new, imaginative creation. (You could also ask, nay insist, that everyone produces attention-grabbing handouts.)

Without exception, the first item on your agenda or schema (that jumped out of the thesaurus as well) should always be humour. This is a sure fire way to get everything off to a good start.

Ask (a polite way of demanding) a different person each time to get the ball rolling with a funny yarn or a quick joke. And don't let the timid ones off – write it into their job description – after they've signed their Contract!

And what about those latecomers? Have you noticed that they're usually the same people every time? It's tantamount to a theatrical encore.

And the excuses that these folk hand out – the last minute critical telephone call; stuck behind a tractor; the dentist had mislaid his drill...!! Oh, how I wish ...

Okay. Here's your chance, Mr Chairman (whoops – chairperson, must be politically correct here). What a great time you can have creating amusing forfeits for latecomers. (No, not that one. That's more for the New Year's Eve party after a glass or two).

Remember, always, to finish these things as they began – with humour. Send folk away laughing – so they'll eagerly look forward to the next time.

By the way

Have you been holding your meetings (I can hardly bear to write that word) in the Boardroom? Hey, come on folk, give this location a bright, new name. How can you possibly expect your guys to get motivated and fired up with inspiration in a Bored Room?

On those really nice summer days, try meeting up in the park with a bottle of bubbly; on those not-so-nice days find a quiet corner in the bar of a country pub. (Drivers on the orange juice, of course.)

Gently does it though

Take great care that you don't ban something to the recycling dungeon before you've examined the situation from every angle. A new slant, a bit of tweaking here and there, is often all that's necessary to boost the pizzazz.

Banning the boring does not mean eliminating anything that has the potential to become boring because, obviously, most things present that possibility. Therefore, only ban the boring because you, other people, and preferably a grand total of everyone, are of the opinion that you are great big, empire-state-building, bored.

Are you keeping up with my gibberings?

Always be aware that boredom is an insidious affliction that has the vindictive ability to silently chip its way into the nooks and crannies of both the mind and the workplace.

So, constantly be on the lookout for ways of putting a new slant on 'the old routine' and I reckon you could be very surprised at how much is achieved with only a nudge here and there; just being in a different, more relaxed atmosphere for example, can work wonders.

My friends, there are umpteen ways to make changes that create fun and laughter in your workplace; ideas that will ensure that your organisation becomes a boomerang of creative interaction, with innovative thoughts bubbling like fresh coffee in a percolator.

Take a look at chapter 9 where I give you lots of ideas for cranking up the company's crazy humour system.

Having ordinary fun doing extraordinary things is good.

Once you get humour buzzing in your workplace, you'll be having extraordinary fun doing ordinary things.

And that feels bloomin' wonderful!

The trick is to experiment until you find what works in your organisation.

**Good Leaders do it with fun –
seriousness is derelict behaviour.**

**A spirited organisation sees more than ghosts –
it's forward thinking.**

Humour diminishes hostility and tension, and provides a cornucopia of relief.

Laughter invigorates meetings and creates a boomerang of lively interaction.

Balderdash supports dynamic thinking and encourages innovative ideas.

**Laughter is a stress management tool –
ridiculously successful.**

5

It's Jester Thought

It's no joke

Have you ever found yourself in the company of an amateur 'professional joker'? – one of those people who reels off joke after joke and thinks he's the world's gift to fun and laughter?

Mmm ... and did you find yourself splitting your sides with laughter initially and, after a while, strangely desperate to get away because ...

... it wasn't your sides that were splitting. It was your head!

Okay ... jokes are great. Just keep a tight rein on 'em!

A workforce of joking jesters is a shortcut to a workforce of zizzing zombies – because employee's basic needs will simply not be met.

(Do you remember reading that bit about basic needs? Or did you think I'd just thrown it in for fun? Remember, every seemingly unimportant word in this book has a serious important meaning).

Here's what I'd like you to do
I'm urging you to encourage light-hearted banter and easy, teasing, chitchat in the workplace. And to laugh at yourself! It's impossible to stress the importance of this too much, or repeat it too often. The more you laugh at your own shortcomings, the better people will respond to you. Self-deprecating comments work wonders, I assure you.

Only recently, I was taken to dinner at a delightful French Bistro in Bath. My colleague and I were enjoying coffee after a superb meal and I glanced at the photographs on the wall behind me.

'*Oh, is that Blackpool Tower?*' I asked, with less intelligence than a plastic spoon.

My companion kept a straight face and tactfully replied, '*I don't think so.*'

I then realised how dim-witted I'd been. A photograph of Blackpool Tower in a French Bistro? I sure was on the back row when brains were handed out. Of course, it had to be the Eiffel Tower.

When the waitress came back I laughingly told her about my faux pas. (Thought I'd impress you with my French). Because I was laughing at my own stupidity, it gave her permission to laugh too. And my companion. And the party at the next table. And, pretty soon, everyone in the Bistro was having a good laugh at my expense. It felt just wonderful, and was, also, the beginning of a couple of new friendships.

I guarantee that you, and your workforce, will always work a whole lot better when you're enjoying yourselves.

'Having fun @ work rules. OK?'

Consider this for innovative, fun, thinking for success

The following is an actual question given on the University of Liverpool's chemistry finals paper. The answer by one student was so 'profound' that the professor shared it with colleagues via the Internet, which is why we now have the pleasure of enjoying it as well.

Bonus Question: Is Hell exothermic (gives off heat) or endothermic (absorbs heat)?

Most of the students wrote proofs of their beliefs using Boyle's Law that gas cools when it expands and heats when it is compressed, or some variant. One student, however, wrote the following:

It's Jester Thought

First, we need to know how the mass of Hell is changing in time. So we need to know the rate at which souls are moving into Hell and the rate at which they are leaving. I think that we can safely assume that once a soul gets to Hell, it will not leave. Therefore, no souls are leaving.

As for how many souls are entering Hell, let's look at the different religions that exist in the world today. Most of these religions state that if you are not a member of their religion, you will go to Hell.

Since there is more than one of these religions, and since people do not belong to more than one religion, we can project that all souls go to Hell. With birth and death rates as they are, we can expect the number of souls in Hell to increase exponentially.

Now, we look at the rate of change of the volume in Hell. Because Boyle's Law states that in order for the temperature and pressure in Hell to stay constant, the volume of Hell must expand proportionately as souls are added

This gives two possibilities:

1. If Hell is expanding at a slower rate than the rate at which souls enter Hell, then the temperature and pressure in Hell will increase until all Hell breaks loose.

2. If Hell is expanding at a rate faster than the increase of souls in Hell, then the temperature and pressure will drop until Hell freezes over.

So which is it?

If we accept the postulate given to me by Sandra during my freshman year that 'it will be a cold day in Hell before I sleep with you,' and take into account the fact that I slept with her last night, then number 2 must be true, and thus I am sure that Hell is endothermic and has already frozen over.

The corollary of this theory is that since Hell has frozen over, it follows that it is not accepting any more souls and is extinct ... leaving only Heaven, thereby proving the existence of a divine being – which explains why, last night, Sandra kept shouting, 'Oh, my God.'

This student received the only 'A'.

Dismiss the solemnity belief

You should now be well and truly convinced of the importance of dispelling the wide belief that it's necessary to be solemn in order to be taken seriously. The fact is, as the above example demonstrates, you can get a serious point across, much better, with a splash of humour.

Humour is the lubricant that helps the content go down

Fun and laughter are guaranteed to lighten tense situations by throwing a ridiculous spanner into serious works. This important tool should be in the armoury of all devotees of successful business.

As soon as this atmosphere-changing tool is tossed into the fray, a lighter mood emerges and new ideas begin to flow – ideas that never would have seen the light of day, in a more serious mood.

So, my friends ...

Take time to laugh – it is the music of the soul.
                                      from an old English prayer

... dismiss the green fly in your life with a flourish of your personal insecticide spray; take time to smell the roses; and let nothing dampen your mood as you allow your mind to drift and consider life in the fast lane. This is the place, is it not, where many tireless workers have their offices?

I should mention at this point, although for no other reason than I rather fancy mentioning it, that I no longer have an office. Sadly, it developed 'sick building syndrome.'

I turned up, as usual, at 9am one morning, only to find that my office building had disappeared. And not a shred of evidence to say that it had even existed. No bits of cement, door latches, or remains of a false eyelash anywhere.

I was totally bereft and worried to a frazzle as I hunted high and low for my office. Eventually, I made my way to the police station to report it missing and a posse was immediately organised to search the area.

By this time, the butterflies in my tummy were flying in glorious formation.

Then, well ... I could hardly believe it, my office called me on my mobile telephone ... *to say it had a migraine!* A classic symptom, it stated, of workplace stress. It began quoting me Japanese terms, like *karoshi*, which, by the way, made me mentally question the severity of the migraine.

Karoshi, my supposedly sick office went on to explain, (as my reputation and career shuddered under the withering gaze of the duty officer), loosely translates to 'death by overwork.' Apparently, during the stress decade of the 1980s, more than 10,000 Japanese executives a year were thought to be dying due to *karoshi*.

Of course, if you're not Japanese, this snippet of information might be of little interest to you. However, if you're in management, anywhere, it should be. So take note, dead employees do not contribute to your bottom line. Obvious? Then why aren't more people getting the message eh?

So, as I stood in the police station, listening to this diatribe from an office that was clearly milking the situation for all it was worth, I made the decision that I would work from home in future.

Some frank rubbish

Let's speak frankly here. I can have fun writing rubbish from anywhere and, ooooh, I like it ... I can sit and look quizzically at my computer for hours and nobody even notices.

Aha! That's because nobody can see me!

'That's obvious!'

Did I really hear you say that? Now, steady on there, don't speak so harshly, so quickly. Things are not always as they seem.

I've had my share of Monday – Friday 9 – 5 jobs that stretched into endless Monday – Sunday 7 – 11 jobs, with a tomato sandwich on the hoof for lunch and an empty fridge and an ancient copy of *Hello* to welcome me home. I've also lost copious amounts of night's sleep through worrying about work.

Now, it was the day I caught myself sending copies of my emails to the Queen, telephoning the Pope to order stationery and inviting Genghis Khan to be guest of honour at our end of conference dinner that I decided insanity was not for me.

It took me no time at all to type out my resignation – in 36 font; red, bold and underlined – and I hastily pushed it to the bottom of my MD's (duh) pending tray (Ha Ha! By the time he got around to reading it, I would have worked out my month's notice; claiming to have been working out of the country at the time).

I donned my bright yellow, over-sized, knee length plastic mackintosh with tartan lined hood, rushed out of the building and jumped on a number 47 red double-decker bus going to Clapham. Fortunately for me, it was just passing by and, even more fortunately, I happened to live in Clapham.

Unfortunately, however, the driver had forgotten to change the destination sign on the front of the bus and it transpired that he was actually transporting a group of strippers to perform in a nightclub in Llandudno.

I know you will appreciate my feelings, when I say that I felt distinctly out of place in this gathering. No newly coiffered hair framed my flustered brow; my lipstick was smudged up my nose and my eyelashes hadn't been curled in weeks.

So, for the second time in the space of half an hour, I quit. I leapt from the bus at it slowed down at red traffic lights and began my long walk home to Clapham.

Of course, my story is by no means unique. Folk quit their jobs every day. Okay, they don't usually mimic an orphan daffodil jumping on and off a number 47 bus – though I'm sure you get my drift.

It's all about what stress can do to us and how it can be avoided. Remember, prevention is better than cure. Or, in other words, *'If you're really serious about your business, then you can't be really serious.'*

So, readers, this brings us back to using humour, and its resultant laughter, as an antidote for stress. And the reason it works? Because having a sense of humour is the direct opposite of having a feeling of being stressed.

Pump up those arteries, folk

According to the findings of a research team from the University of Maryland School of Medicine, Baltimore, USA, stress causes blood flow to slow down around 35%, whilst laughter increases the flow by something like 22%.

These research guys apparently studied the reactions that folk had when watching funny films compared with stressful films.

So, lets not waste the time of these clever guys, eh? Let's put their valuable findings into action and get laughing.

Get your chuckle zone revved up again with these humorous business advertisements.

Chucklesome ads

Electrician's van:	Let us look into your shorts
Butcher's window:	I'll always meat your needs
Vet's waiting room:	I'll be back in 10 minutes. Sit! Stay!
On a fence:	Salesmen very welcome. Cheaper than dog food
Hotel window:	We need inn-experienced people. Apply within
Electricity company:	We would be de-lighted if you paid your account

**Words + People + Places + Imagination
can create such a lot of fun**

6

A Happenstance a Day Keeps the Doctor Away

Happenstance (Plural: Happenstances) is such a descriptive word, don't you think? One that so cleverly takes happenings, incidents and instances and embraces them under one big 'happenstance' umbrella.

So, here are a few humorous ...

Miscellaneous happenstance ramblings

My two daughters have been dining out on my mishaps for over thirty years. (I admit it, I am that old; and the drinks are on you if you ever mention it again). And this is a good time to mention that family members can usually take a bit of ribbing. Because of the delicate social dynamics that exist in the workplace, (I'll say it again) please, do avoid making comments that may belittle people.

Back to my two girls. They still laugh about the time I put paprika in the Christmas cake instead of mixed spice ...

Hey, you're not supposed to laugh! This is a serious matter and, anyway, paprika pepper and mixed spice look much the same to me without my specs – though, now, I admit I wasn't even aware I needed them, never mind wasn't wearing them.

It didn't take number one daughter long to work out what I'd done. I'd like to think that it was her high IQ that made her so quick on the uptake, though I suspect the burning sensation in her mouth must have been one huge clue.

Then there was the time I forgot to put the curry powder in the curry. The pizzazz was kinda missing – still, it was a mighty fine tasting casserole!

How about this one then

I have a friend who is a financial consultant (yes, really) and he works in a 'goldfish bowl' of an office. On this particular day – being financial, he's very particular about his days – he was working on his computer and so, naturally, he had to gaze at the screen a lot. After a while, he got so mesmerised by row – upon row – upon row – of figures, that he just dropped down into a very deep trance.

The guy in the office across the glass corridor (different company, so no direct access, apart from breaking the glass) could see my friend, in his 'goldfish bowl' office, and noticed that he hadn't moved for about three hours. So, Mr Concerned from across the corridor, telephoned the police and said:

'I think the guy in a nearby office has had a heart attack, he's just sitting in front of his computer staring at the screen. He hasn't moved for about three hours.'

The outcome of this was that my financial friend was roused from his hypnotic trance by two policemen, Mr Concerned from across the way and a couple of ambulance guys rushing into his office, complete with stretcher, portable resuscitator and a collection box for The British Heart Foundation.

….. and all ended happily and laughingly.

Here comes another story from my financial friend ...

He had two appointments in close succession.

The first appointment was with a guy who turned up very late; and the second appointment was with a guy who turned up very early.

Now, Mr Financial Friend, never having previously met either Mr Appointment (1) or Mr Appointment (2), and with his secretary on holiday, mistook one guy for the other.

Are you keeping up with me here?

Okay. Mr Financial Friend, already being in possession of completed application forms from Mr Appointment (1) and Mr Appointment (2), detailing a miscellany of personal information, cheerily shook the hand of (2) believing him to be (1) and invited him into his office, gave him a cup of coffee and proceeded thus:

FF	*You are forty eight years old?*
Appt 2	*Yes, I am.*
FF	*And although you've had problems with raised blood pressure, your medical report states that things have stabilised.*
Appt 2	*Yes, I'm fine now.*
FF	*That's good. And you've recently moved house?*
Appt 2	*Yes.*
FF	*And how are your wife and children liking their new home?*
Appt 2	*I don't have a wife. I think you've got the wrong person.*
FF	*And I think it's important to see the funny side of embarrassing situations. Do you agree?*

… and all ended happily and laughingly.

My PR friend still laughs about this

My PR friend started his career working in 10 Downing Street and, as a raw recruit, he was attempting very hard to impress a well known QC over the telephone.

QC	*Can you send the papers round to me?*
Friend	*Certainly, I'll get a courier to bring them round to you immediately.*
Courier	(Reading address on envelope and rolling around laughing) *The QC's Chambers are in Grays Inn Road, not 'Grazing Road'.*

I should hastily point out that my friend now heads his own highly successful PR Company. To put his new recruits at ease, he relates his 'Grazing Road' story. He also lends them his tatty A-Z of London!

This reminds me of the inexperienced reporter writing about a famous American author having just been awarded the 'Pullet Surprise' … or the young child, happy to sing the hymn about 'Gladly, my cross-eyed bear'.

This story comes from Malcolm

Malcolm is my British friend who now lives in France. He warns of the dangers of even slightly mis-pronouncing words.

Malcolm's neighbour, Paul, developed a painful, stiff neck after cleaning the beams in his farmhouse. He consulted a French dictionary and found that 'painful' was 'mal' and 'neck' was 'cou'.

Confident in his mastery of the subject, Paul trotted off to the local docteur who (unusually, I'm told) did not speak any English.

Paul explained to the docteur that he had 'mal de cou' whereupon the docteur signalled to him to drop his trousers and pants. The docteur then proceeded, after donning rubber gloves, to give a full rectal examination. Paul thought this was a bit strange, but thought that the docteur knew something he didn't.

Eventually, the docteur straightened up and indicated that he could find nothing wrong; whereupon Paul rubbed his neck and said that it was still a problem.

The docteur then saw the light and fell about laughing, with tears running down his cheeks. He explained to Paul that, unless pronounced with scrupulous accuracy, the word for neck 'cou' could easily be mistaken for 'cul' meaning backside, bottom or buttocks (I'm attempting to be polite here), according to intonation.

Another story from my friend, Malcolm, in France

A local councillor, Pierre, who is a retired, harmless looking farmer aged 80+, invited my friend around for an aperitif.

Pierre told Malcolm he'd lived in that area all his life and had, in fact, been a member of the resistance during the war. When Malcolm suggested he could only have been a schoolboy, Pierre said:

'That's right, but I still had two revolvers, like Clint Eastwood, and used to take messages from the town to the Maquisades in the forest.'

Q: With this kind of back-up, were we lucky not to have been invaded?

This also came from Malcolm in France. I don't where it was before then. Thank you to whoever created this incredible rubbish.

I cdnuolt blveiee that I cluod aulaclty uesdnatnrd what I was rdanieg. The phaonmneal pweor of the huamn mind, aoccdrnig to a rseearerch at Cmabrigde Uinervtisy, it deosn't mttaer in what order the ltteers in a word are, the only iprmoatnt thing is that the frist and lsat ltteer be in the rghit pclae.

The rset can be a taotl mses and you can still raed it wouthit a porbelm. This is bcuseae the human mind deos not raed ervey lteter by istlef, but the word as a wlohe. Amzanig huh? Yaeh, and I awlyas tghuhot slpeling was ipmorantt!

Did you have fun deciphering the gobbledegook?

Or do you reckon it's kinda sad when bad things happen to good sentences?

Friend with injured leg

I have a dear friend, John, who injured his leg rather badly whilst playing tennis. Throughout the entire lengthy and painful recovery period, however, John always maintained his sense of humour.

Over the telephone one day, John told me that the only place he could manage to get any relief from the wretched pain in his leg was in a lovely warm bath.

Always eager to see the funny side of things, John laughingly remarked:

'What I really need is a suit of armour – then I can put warm water in the legs and walk around in it all day.'

2006 – World Cup time again

As I write this book, it's wall-to-wall football.

Okay, for football fans this is a frenetic time, with nails chewed to the quick. For those folk who are loyal anti-football fans, it's a totally different state of affairs.

As my dear friend, Gwyneth, puts it:

'(Her) favourite television programmes are either moved to different times or are abandoned altogether so that 22 legs running around can be broadcast live.'

Shades of Shakespeare

I have a couple of lads installing my conservatory. They're identical twins called Mark and Anthony. *'From Julius Caeser,'* Anthony explained. *'Mark was born first, then me, Anthony.'*

Musical comedy

My much-valued friend, Kevin Bowyer, a brilliant and internationally renowned organist, has a keen sense of humour. When interviewed by the press, reporters are usually taken by surprise when they encounter Kevin's quick responses to their serious questions, e.g.:

    Q *'What are your main loves?'*
    KB *'Real ale and malt whisky.'*
    Q *'What is your favourite occupation?'*
    KB *'Sleeping.'*

Laugh or you'll cry

The wife behind the job

I was married to an RAF Officer and when he was stationed at Brampton in Huntingdonshire (County boundaries have since been changed and it's now in Cambridgeshire) I joined a group called The Parkside Players.

We were a talented collection of entertainers from all three services (say I modestly) – serving men and women and family members, actors, magicians, singers, musicians, comedians – plus backstage helpers, stagehands, electricians – well, anyone we could rope in – and we travelled around, lugging all our gear in an RAF truck, to entertain whoever asked us, (charitable organisations, senior citizens's clubs etc) entirely free of charge and for the pure love of it.

We had a wonderful time and performed in some 'unusual' venues. Often, there were no proper changing room facilities so, enthusiastic and undaunted, the guys used to string up a couple of parachutes and create a makeshift one.

We'd been doing this for years when a guy came up after the show and said:

'Did you know you can see right through those parachutes when the lights are on ... ???'

Moving on

From Brampton, my husband was then posted to Cosford in Shropshire. And I missed the fun, laughter and tremendous camaraderie of The Parkside Players enormously, so I joined a local amateur operatic society.

I was lucky enough to be given the part of Elsie, the leading soprano in Yeoman of the Guard. Rehearsals were a bundle of fun and production week was going swimmingly until, during the third night of the production, a button on my costume got entangled with the leading man's jacket during a duet.

What a fiasco!

We endeavoured to sing on through our giggles, holding each other ridiculously close and frantically trying to untangle ourselves without anyone noticing. Not a chance.

Our predicament was, by now, obvious to everyone – the whole cast, backstage and front of house crew; and the entire audience – were all in fits of laughter. Not laughing at us – with us!

And, so, breaking with true show business tradition – the show just did not go on.

Someone appeared with a pair of scissors and cut us free; the audience gave a rousing hand of applause worthy of an encore for any West End production; the orchestra recovered and blew, bowed and drummed their way into the next number; our costumes were later repaired by a most able seamstress; and we received the most fantastic review in our local newspaper.

'Never,' wrote the reporter, *'have I enjoyed myself more, and been witness to such a great sense of fun and professionalism, than that which rescued this very difficult situation.'*

The Council Tax man

Since the early 1990s, I've enjoyed renovating property. One of my greatest challenges has been a Victorian cottage that I literally took apart and put back together again – and lived in the place throughout!

Wow, roughing it is an understatement!

During the restoration of the lounge, I asked the builders to remove the ghastly modern fireplace that a previous owner had installed and knock down the wall, because I had a hunch that an old inglenook was hidden behind it. (I was mistaken, though it was fun finding out.)

Well, I'm sure you can picture the kind of a mess this undertaking presented and the amount of rubble it created – and it was all piled in the middle of the lounge floor ... when the Council Tax man knocked on my door. Leastways, he would have knocked had there been a door. That had been temporarily removed to get a rather large generator through. You've got it – no electricity.

Anyway, Mr Council Tax man explained that he was just making a routine call, though I never did ascertain how or why this came about. Very odd – I'd filled in all the relevant forms.

'Where are you living whilst the building work is being carried out?' I was asked. (Was this just idle curiosity, I wondered, though decided to let it pass.)

'Here,' I said.

Mr Council Tax man stood with one foot resting on the pile of debris. Wiping the dust from his brow, he looked around in awe and his eyes glazed over in amazement as he uttered the immortal words:

'But it's totally uninhabitable.'

We laughed, with amusement on his part and more like frustration on mine, as I was told that there would be no reduction in Council Tax for residing in an 'uninhabitable' house.

John F Kennedy

Whilst campaigning in West Virginia for the presidency, John F Kennedy was speaking to a group of coal miners.

'What do you know about our situation?' shouted one miner. *'You haven't worked a day in your life.'*

'It's true.' Senator Kennedy humbly replied.

'That's OK,' another miner said. *'You haven't missed anything.'*

Miscellaneous stories and one-liners

A young executive was leaving the office late one evening when he found the CEO standing in front of the shredder with a piece of paper in his hand.

'*Listen,*' said the CEO, '*this is a very sensitive and important document here and my secretary has gone for the night. Can you make this machine work?*'

'*Certainly,*' said the young executive.

He turned on the machine, inserted the paper and pressed the start button.

'*Excellent, excellent,*' said the CEO as his paper disappeared inside the shredder. '*I just need one copy.*'

----------------------o-------------------

Notice in window of local council office

'Wanted – beds for the homeless'

(Just where did they intend putting these beds?)

----------------------o-------------------

Never drink black coffee at lunch; it will keep you awake all afternoon.

Jilly Cooper, writer

----------------------o-------------------

They announced on US TV that Patrick McNee, star of The Avengers, had died. His daughter was contacted in Palm Springs.

'*Sorry to hear that your father's dead*'
'*But I was talking to him 12 minutes ago in Australia,*'
'*No, he's dead – it's just the time difference.*'

Patrick McNee, actor

----------------------o-------------------

Birth was the death of him.
Samuel Becket, playwright

She looked as if she'd been poured into her clothes and had forgotten to say 'when'.
P.G. Wodehouse, writer

In 1823, William Webb Ellis first picked up the ball in his arms and ran with it. And for the next 156 years, forwards have been trying to work out why.
Tasker Watkins, President of the Welsh Rugby Union

I love deadlines. I especially like the whooshing sound they make as they go flying by.
Douglas Adams

The only reason I made a commercial for American Express was to pay for my American Express bill.
Peter Ustinov

I'm having so much fun, I feel guilty taking your money ... but I will ...
Liberace

A Happenstance a Day Keeps the Doctor Away

How long was I in the army? Five foot eleven.
                                    Spike Milligan, comedian

---o---

If you are going to tell people the truth, you had better make them laugh. Otherwise they'll kill you.
                                    George Bernard Shaw

---o---

A wise man will live as much within his wit as within his income.
                                    Lord Chesterfield, politician

---o---

Having accepted the waiter's offer of a glass of wine, a young delegate attending his first conference banquet heard a bishop on a nearby table decline a similar invitation by declaring:
  'I would sooner commit adultery than partake of alcohol.'
  Turning to his more immediate neighbour, the young delegate remarked:
  'I didn't realise we had a choice.'

---o---

More and more, these days, I find myself pondering how to reconcile my net income with my gross habits.
                                    John Nelson

---o---

Gentlemen prefer bonds.
                                    Andrew Mellon

---o---

> *I told the Inland Revenue that I didn't owe them a penny because I lived near the seaside.*
> — Ken Dodd

> *We didn't actually overspend our budget. The allocation simply fell short of our expenditure.*
> — Keith Davis

> *If you owe the bank $100 that's your problem; if you owe the bank $100 million, that's the bank's problem.*
> — J. P. Getty

> *I've got all the money I'll ever need if I die by four o' clock this afternoon.*
> — Henry Youngman

> *Anyone who lives within their means suffers from a lack of imagination.*
> — Oscar Wilde

Unaccustomed as I am ...

Bits from me ... and ... bits from them

The successful entrepreneur was constantly in demand for after-dinner speeches and could never find the time to prepare his own material. It would always be his assistant who wrote the speech.

It was at the annual conference that he was called upon to give encouragement to small businesses. After the meal, the entrepreneur stood up to address the audience.
 'Ladies and Gentlemen.
 There are three main areas of tension in today's small business. The first is the problem of not paying competitive salaries ...'
 He then turned to the next page and read out,
 'From now on, you unappreciative pig, you're on your own ...'
Pam Brown

---------------------O-------------------

There are two things that are more difficult than making an after-dinner speech; climbing a wall that is leaning toward you and kissing a girl who is leaning away from you.
Sir Winston Churchill

---------------------O-------------------

Two elderly ladies were listening to the speech given after the charity dinner they attended every year. After some time, one of them, who was extremely hard of hearing, whispered loudly to the other:
 'Hasn't he finished yet?'
 'Oh yes,' answered her friend. 'He's finished. He just doesn't seem able to stop.'
Peter Grey

---------------------O-------------------

At a banquet given by Arthur Rank of Pinewood Studios, one of the after-dinner speakers went on and on.
 A E Mathews, in a very loud voice, proclaimed:
 'Good God, doesn't the fellow know I haven't got long to live.'

---------------------O-------------------

The main guest speaker (replying for the guests) had gone on (mostly about himself) for some thirty-five minutes.

The Master (in the Chair) then rose to close the evening's proceedings. He said:
'I'm sure I speak for all when I say how greatly we enjoyed Sir Billhook's moving and comprehensive address. We really must remember to ask him again – when he has less time ...'
Sir Desmond Heap, from *My Lords, Ladies and Gentlemen*

----------------------o-------------------

I asked your chairperson for details of the people I would be speaking to today – numbers, broken down by age and sex – and he replied: 'Yes, they are ...'
Clement Freud

----------------------o-------------------

The US President, Theodore Roosevelt, was asked how long it took him to prepare one of his speeches. His reply was that it depended on the length of the speech required; for a half-an-hour speech, two to three days, for five minutes, a week and if he had to speak for two hours then he could begin immediately.

----------------------o-------------------

Speaking to you tonight reminds me of the American professor of Nuclear Physics who, as well as his duties as a Departmental Head, undertook a wide series of visiting lectures.

Being driven one afternoon by his chauffeur to a lecture engagement at a University, a conversation developed when the chauffeur commented upon the unfairness of life; he was paid a paltry few thousand dollars per annum, whereas the professor, no doubt, received a large salary and substantial sums for his lecture engagements.

When the professor mentioned that this was a reflection of their relative abilities, the chauffeur politely remonstrated:

'Rubbish – he had sat at the back of the hall, heard this, and many

other lectures, such that he could do it without a problem, particularly with the aid of slides.'

'Stop the car,' said the professor, *'let us change places and you can give this evening's lecture.'*

Having been duly received by the Dean of the University, the chauffeur gave a splendid lecture, with many gestures and learned quips, such that he received a standing ovation.

In his vote of thanks, the Dean of the Faculty mentioned that he had assembled many of his most able research workers, anxious to ask questions.

The chauffeur agreed, after a moment's hesitation, to take questions. A most earnest young man asked:

'What were the professor's views on the structure of the negative proton?'

Taken aback, the chauffeur paused and replied slowly:

'This is a most elementary, dare I say even a naïve question. It is, in fact, so simple that I will ask my chauffeur, sitting in the back of the hall, to answer it.'

David Atterton, from *My Lords, Ladies and Gentlemen*

7

Doin' It Your Way

And which way might that be?

Before everything, and above all, in order to enjoy your work, you must be in the right vocation for you; one that's suited to your personality and keenly tuned to your abilities.

Let's be clear here. There is absolutely no point whatsoever in attempting to turn an unsuitable job, in an incompatible environment, into a stable, playful and permanent experience. Although laughter will certainly generate a temporary reprieve, it's merely wishful thinking to expect it to create anything more permanent.

Therefore, the basis of having fun at work is doing a job that you're nutty about; one that fulfils you and gives you a passionate glow in the cockles of your heart just by thinking about it.

To get to this point, it's necessary to:

- identify your wants, needs and goals (bear in mind that these are not the same as dreams and wishes)
- ascertain how and where and when you can achieve these
- determine the right route to attaining them, put yourself on it and stay on it
- continually check your course to see if you need to make changes
- correct your pathway if you feel you're off course
- frequently check that you are moving towards your goal
- ... and be determined to reach it!

Lighten your darkness

Your true pathway, the one that you were born to follow, is written in the stars. Yes, really!

So, readers, it's good to tweak your ears and listen well and hard to the universe. It knows all the important details of your life; what makes you happy; and the things that cause you pain; the sort of work that consistently fires you with enthusiasm and drives you to achieve; and what kind of jobs will always fill you with dismay and force you to clock-watch.

The universe knows which is the right pathway for you and, believe me, if you're not on it, you're destined for a life of miserable hard grind.

Okay. You've listened and, hopefully, know where your pathway should be leading you. Now, it's time to get up on your toes and be ready, willing and ever so able to let the universe guide you down the road towards the happy, successful and prosperous life you were born to live; that enjoyable, fulfilling and meaningful existence you were meant to follow – the one that's been written in the stars from the moment you came hollering, screaming and kicking into this thing called life.

Nooooo!, I'm not talking astrologically

I'm talking about a physically planned pathway for your future – one that you instinctively know is right for you. And that means you've found your real purpose in life (your destiny, call it what you will). You can see, hear and feel it, and know, beyond a shadow of doubt, how you want your life to be. And, you know, achieving that goal is really easy, because you were born with the ability to achieve it.

You will know when you've got there – when you've reached your ultimate goal – because you will feel that you have:

- fulfilled the highest possibilities within your life.
- made your finest contribution to society and the world
- achieved and enjoyed your greatest results.

Now! What could be better than that?

Your personal pathway

Any five year-old will tell you that finding your personal pathway is easy peasy. You simply work at what gives you the greatest pleasure and the most happiness and, hey, you've found your true pathway.

However, as you're no longer five years old (I assume) and maybe feeling unhappy and unfulfilled in your job, it's unlikely that you're going to agree with the thinking of a five year-old. Ooooh no, no, no, life's had too much of a go at you!

It is likely, though, if you're dissatisfied with your working life, that you need to consider making some changes.

You, may, of course, be on your true pathway and working with others that aren't. Therefore, you're not linked with like-minded people in an atmosphere of incompatibility and harmony.

It could be that simple. Or not. Whatever, it's important that you determine what you are; where you are; what you want; and how you can achieve it. Then go for the fun of it!

Move along now
It's important to remember that the universe is not static. It's free floating and moves for you and with you; constantly inspiring, motivating, fulfilling your passions; and firing your enthusiasm for day to day opportunities and challenges.

If your days are not fulfilling, or have ceased to be as meaningful as they once were, here are ten pointers to consider.

1. What are the areas in which you excel?
2. What things feel 'easy' in your life?
3. What are your passions?
4. What is important to you?
5. What makes you want to get up in the morning?
6. What gives your life fulfilment and meaning?
7. What inspires and motivates you?
8. What fires you with enthusiasm?
9. What do you enjoy so much that you forget all sense of time?
10. What makes you feel needed, loved and valued?

When you have a clear answer to the above ten questions, you are now in a position where you can start to move your life in the direction of your identified needs.

In other words, you lay your fire; you light it; and you just carry on stoking it with the right fuel.

When is a job not just a job?

... when you're passionate about what you do. When your occupation is you; and you give of yourself freely and completely to be, and to do, what you really are. You are being, doing and feeling the sort of person that the universe created you to be.

----------------------o-------------------

My entry into music was instinctive. I wasn't choosing anything. I was chosen. I didn't have the choice of shall I be a mathematician, or an instrumentalist, or a teacher? That never occurred to me.
Aaron Copeland, American composer

----------------------o-------------------

'Great minds have purposes, others have wishes.'
Washington Irving, American author

----------------------o-------------------

It's a sad fact of life that most people never bother to identify their real talents.

These folk are so wrapped up in the age-old adage that work and play don't mix, so that they just amble through each working day without giving themselves any chance at all to shine, be happy and have fun.

So, readers, check out your talents. Are you working with them or against them?

Life is what happens to us while we're busy making other plans.
John Lennon

It's a fact
Oh so many people get permanently imprisoned in a state of 'having to work' instead of 'loving to work.' How easy it is to unwittingly condemn oneself to a working (and personal) life of frustration and unfulfilled, meaningless days of boredom and resentment.

If you're on this pathway folk – jump off it pronto! But not until you've carefully considered where you're going to land. Going from the frying pan into the fire is not a good idea. And, remember, love does not pay the bills!

Wanna live longer?
Research has shown that active people, with a purpose in life, live longer. And here's another interesting fact. Joy slows down the ageing process.

Again, the message from the universe is loud, clear and very strong.

Get paid for doing what gives you the greatest pleasure; creates buckets full of happiness for you; fills your heart with much joy; and gives you the opportunity to stick around on this earth much longer to enjoy it

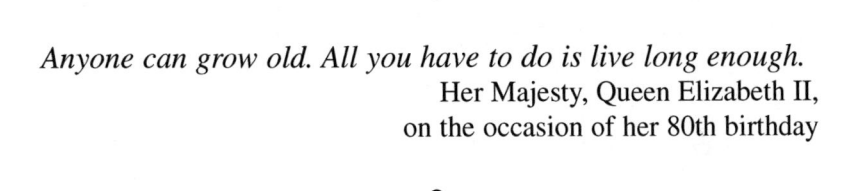

---------------------O-------------------

Anyone can grow old. All you have to do is live long enough.
Her Majesty, Queen Elizabeth II,
on the occasion of her 80th birthday

---------------------O-------------------

Benefits of enjoying what you do

When your work equals a time of play, fun and laughter, adequate

financial remuneration will invariably follow – because you will be giving of your very best.

And, as I said previously, you will have a far greater chance of living longer to reap the rewards.

Laughs a day keep the doctor at bay

More Chuckles

- Enraged cow injures farmer with axe
- Plane too close to ground, crash probe told
- Juvenile court to try shooting defendant
- Stolen painting found by tree
- Two soviet ships collide, one dies
- Killer sentenced to die for second time in ten years
- War dims hope for peace
- If strike isn't settled quickly, it may last a while
- Cold wave linked to temperatures
- Red tape holds up new bridge
- New study of obesity looks for larger test group
- Chef throws his heart into helping feed needy
- Local high school dropouts cut in half.

8

Humour Aerobics

The fun way to a lighter, healthier body

Have you heard the latest news? We have 400 muscles in our body!
  'Ah, but that's not new,' do I hear you exclaim?
  Frankly, for me, it is, having abandoned those supposedly important aspects of my education in favour of enjoying myself.
  I abandoned French in favour of music; statistics in favour of drama; and biology in favour of spotty, lanky boys from the local grammar school.
  Looking back, I'm amazed at the ease with which I made these life-changing decisions. Maybe it was easier because I made them without my parents' consent (even their knowledge), come to think about it. I wasn't rebellious, merely tweaking life to make it more fun. And, in order to do that, I definitely didn't need to know how many muscles there were in my body!
  Now, amusingly, I hear:
  'There's more to them there muscles than meets the eye.'
  After successfully laughing myself through several decades, I've learnt that I've inadvertently been using all of my 400 muscles well and wisely. Extensive medical research has concluded that it's possible to use every one of the muscles in your body every time you laugh…
  Yes, that's right, every single one of your muscles – face and body – can be used every single time you laugh.
  Incredible. Just think, if you belly-laughed for an hour, that would

mean you could laugh away around 500 calories. Okay, I accept that's a lot of laughing in one go and you do, somehow, need to slot some more serious types of play into the day ...

... so, you just prescribe yourself many smaller doses of 'humour aerobics.'

A bit of maths: 100 laughs equates to 10 minutes of jogging and a good 20 second laugh is the equivalent to 3 minutes on a rowing machine. I'll let you work out how many calories you'd lose – I abandoned maths in favour of life-survival.

Think about this

Humour aerobics needs no special equipment and it's sugar free, fat free, tax free and, frankly, addictive!!

And the effects of a good laugh – being more alert, cheerful, lively – can last for up to 24 hours.

Surveys tell us that, on average, adults laugh 10 to 15 times a day. Not a lot when you consider that a four-year old child laughs an average of 500 times a day. When did we learn to become so serious??

So, readers ...

Laugh well. Laugh often. Burn off those calories.

Get lighter through laughter.

It's on everyone's lips

This is a good place for some more chuckles. The comments over the page were taken from actual medical records as dictated by physicians.

Medical Chuckles

- By the time he was admitted, his rapid heart had stopped and he was feeling better.
- Patient has chest pain if she lies on her side for over a year.
- On the second day the knee was better and, on the third day, it had completely disappeared.
- The patient has been depressed ever since she began seeing me in 1983.
- Patient was released to outpatient department without dressing.
- Discharge status: Alive, but without permission.
- The patient is tearful and crying constantly. She also appears to be depressed.
- The patient will need disposition and, therefore, we will get Dr. Blank to dispose of him.
- Healthy appearing 69 year-old male, mentally alert, but forgetful.
- The patient refused an autopsy.
- The patient has no history of suicides.
- The patient expired on the floor uneventfully.
- The patient's past medical history has been remarkably insignificant, with only a 40 pound weight gain in the past three days.
- Patient has left his white blood cells at another hospital.
- She slipped on the ice and, apparently, her legs went in separate directions in early December.
- Between you and me, we ought to be able to get this lady pregnant.
- The patient was in his usual state of good health until his airplane ran out of gas and crashed.
- She is numb from her toes down.
- While in the ER, she was examined, X-rated and sent home.
- The skin was moist and dry.
- Occasional, constant, infrequent headaches.
- Patient was alert and unresponsive.
- When she fainted, her eyes rolled around the room.

A merry heart

- ✓ The bible states, *'A merry heart doeth good like a medicine.'*

- ✓ Shakespeare wrote, *'A light heart lives longer.'*

- ✓ Bernie Siegel MD states, *'The simple truth is that happy people generally don't get sick.'*

Because humour ... (as if you didn't know by now) ...

- ✓ **Creates laughter and ...**
- ✓ **Laughter relieves stress and lifts spirits.**
- ✓ **People who laugh together are happier together.**
- ✓ **Laughter strengthens the immune system and improves breathing.**
- ✓ **Happiness and a general sense of well being result from laughter.**
- ✓ **Laughter lowers blood pressure and has good cardiovascular effects.**
- ✓ **Better health reduces absenteeism.**
- ✓ **Reduced absenteeism leads to increased productivity.**
- ✓ **Increased productivity leads to increased profits.**
- ✓ **Increased profits inspire and encourage a sense of well-being.**
- ✓ **Well-being increases motivation.**

9

Jingle Jangle to the Bank

Every business in the UK should consider that a happy workforce is tantamount to the success of that business.
Patricia Hewitt, Minister for Trade and Industry
March 2002

Let's get the bad news out of the way

It's currently estimated that stress in the workplace, and resultant physical, emotional and mental problems, costs British businesses £13 billion ... per year!

Stress has, indeed, taken over from the common cold as the biggest reason for employee absence from work, with an ever-increasing number of people saying that they are stressed.

What is more, there are significantly more types of stress hitting the market than ever before. In addition to the common-or-garden stress, we now have 'the rages':

Road Rage; Air Rage; Drunken Rage; Drug Rage; Underground Rage; Parking Rage; Office Rage; Internet Rage; E-mail Rage; and the one that I only recently heard about – Desk Rage.

These rages are all relatively new on the social and business scene. However, let's be frank. Rage is by no means new. It's just – well – that it seems to have got somewhat outrageous in recent years and the media (is there such a thing as Media Rage?) loses no time in letting us know all about it.

In years gone by, no doubt our Mr Hermit that we talked about in an earlier chapter had to endure Caveman Rage, Harpoon Rage, Bow and Arrow Rage, Spear Rage, and, of course, Wild Animal Rage.

No doubt, in a by-gone era, Ben Hur would have suffered Chariot Rage and chances are that General Custer would have encountered Wagon Rage. In times to come we'll maybe have Pizza Rage, when there's no pepperoni; DVD when the rental guy doesn't have a copy of the latest movie; and we'll just blow our top when the parrot won't say 'Pretty Polly' on the hour, every hour.

Anyhow, irrespective of its disguise, all these new fangled rages have their origin in the same monster – stress.

And what exactly is this thing called stress?

Here's the definition that my battered, well-worn, dictionary gives:

'Pressure or tension or compulsion; when much energy is needed; under or driven by stress'

... which tells us ... absolutely ... zilch! ... because stress is such a personal thing. So, here's my definition.

Stress is when the amount of pressure a person has to handle exceeds his or her ability to successfully cope with it.

So, if you're feeling under pressure, and this stress thing is belligerently trespassing into your life, chances are that:

   (a) you have too much to do and not enough hands or mental capacity to deal with it
   (b) you and the job are incompatible
   (c) you and those around you, are on different planets
   (d) you are letting your home and work life overlap
   (e) in a nutshell, you don't have fun doing what you're doing.

So, what can you do about it? Short of just not appearing for work; quitting your job completely or feigning death?

Well, firstly, I recommend that you avoid the temptation to quit, believing that this will immediately resolve everything. Of course, it may do. However, before taking this step, I suggest that you take the time to go inside of your life and have a long, hard look around.

Being the caring gal that I am, and because it's a 'nice to you day' I've prepared a little questionnaire to help you do this (oh, my, that sounds so serious, don't you think? I'll re-phrase it.) ... I've rattled off a little Fun Hunt with hints and tips to clarify and ease your pressure, whilst staying within the law and maintaining a sufficient level of insanity to enjoy the good life.

Here comes the Fun Hunt – have a go and see what happens

You'll need pen and paper.

1. Write down the things that worry you and cause you stress. Put everything down now – don't skip the small stuff – it could be these tiny niggles that grumble away under the surface that are causing you anxiety.

2. What is the worst that could happen with your present scenario? All things considered, are things really as bad as you first thought?

3. Practice reframing the things that you found stressful in (1). There is a saying: *'It isn't what happens to us that's the problem, it's the way we handle it.'*

    And, because individuals perceive things differently, it's only natural that they will, usually, deal with an identical situation differently. For example, whilst one person may find stroking a baby cheetah exhilarating, another may find it absolutely terrifying.

    It's the same experience folk. If you imagined the cheetah as a prostrate goldfish that's jumped out of its tank, would you regard it to be such a frightening experience?

    You have an allergy to goldfish? Okay, just imagine something else then.

4. Are you getting sufficient sleep? If not, then get some more. Your mind and body experience significant stress through sleep deprivation. It alters the way you think; the way you behave; in fact, it alters your whole demeanour.
    Watch out for the body's warning signals of tiredness:
    - excessive yawning
    - heavy eyelids
    - concentration is difficult
    - waves of tiredness
    - head starts to nod
    - with extreme tiredness, hallucinations are common.

5. Begin, and never stop, to laugh more. Remember, it's been proved that even fake smiling and laughing can give your body the same benefits as the real thing.

6. How's your breathing? Your breath should start in the diaphragm. If it's starting in the upper chest (and you may be experiencing all sorts of inexplicable symptoms) then check out 'Hyperventilation' on page 96. This insidious condition, which is difficult to spot, and usually misunderstood by many, can be very debilitating.

7. Learn a relaxation technique (don't multi-technique; that's less effective) and practise it morning and evening, until it has become second nature to you and you can relax standing on your head. Then you'll be able to do it anywhere and at any time – relax, that is, not stand on your head. Then again, it if makes life more fun and helps you sleep at night ...!!

8. As a PS to (5) above, once you have mastered the relaxation technique, you'll find it easy to take frequent, short mental vacations. Just close your eyes, tell yourself you want to open them after five minutes (or ten, fifteen, or however long you want your cat-nap to last) and your subconscious will learn to wake you after the required time. These breaks are very powerful – Winston

Churchill seems to have survived on them during World War II (best not to let your staff catch you at it!).

9. As a PPS to (5) do, unashamedly, take advantage of every possible opportunity to take breaks throughout the day; resist the temptation to 'eat on the job' or 'work through your coffee and lunch break.' No matter how busy you are, a break (even just a short one in order to stretch your legs and get the blood and oxygen flowing) can keep you more alert, encourage creativity and, ultimately, make you more productive.

10. Keep a watchful eye on what you put into your body. Coffee, coke, chocolate (anything that contains caffeine) plus, of course, all that junk food that can be so tempting, can all contribute to increasing your level of stress.

11. Don't skip meals. To do so runs the risk of lowering your blood sugar levels.

12. Drink lots of water. You'll be amazed at how much better it can make you feel.

13. When things aren't going too well, remind yourself of the attitude of Thomas Edison, the inventor of the electric light bulb. When it was suggested that, after 10,000 failed attempts, he should give up his quest. He replied:

'I have not failed 10,000 times, I have successfully found 10,000 ways that will not work.'

14. Although your working life is very important, (love may make the world go round, but it sure doesn't pay the bills) your personal life is equally important. So, just as you would set goals with your job, do so with your personal life and then give them some priority.

15. Ensure that your goals are realistic.
    - Don't attempt perfection (perfectionists are never happy because it's impossible to achieve such a state).
    - Set achievable goals.
    - Allow yourself sufficient time for jobs. A lot of stress is caused through attempting to achieve too much in too short a time.

16. Leave work at the office. Never, ever, be tempted to take it home with you. When I see men and women carrying briefcases to and from work, I desperately hope they contain really important things like lunch, fruit for a snack, bottled water, a 650 page Mills and Boon epic, latest edition of Private Eye, Vogue magazine, a current copy of racing news... or similar!

17. Create a ritual for leaving the office that enables you to leave all work issues behind. Go through the procedure below, every evening, before you leave the office. Don't be tempted to neglect it. Do it methodically and you will notice how much easier it becomes to separate work from home life.
    Here comes the procedure.

- Tidy your desk. Anything other than telephones, hole puncher, stapler and the like should be put away - neatly - in its proper place.
- Keep a drawer, or a section of cupboard for your 'current projects' so that you can put any files and papers out of sight overnight.
- If you've finished with it - file it or bin it.
- Slowly and methodically open and close every cupboard door and all drawers, including filing cabinets in your office.
- Pick up and replace all telephone receivers.
- Check your diary for the following day's appointments.

- Make a 'to do' list for the next day. If it's Friday, then make a list for the following Monday.
- When you leave your office, close the door firmly behind you.
- Unless your briefcase carries such items, or equivalent, to those in (14) leave it behind and only use it for meetings, etc.

On a broader front

- Take up a relaxing hobby; join an art class, yoga group, model aircraft group, flower arranging; anything that is totally unrelated to your job and that gives you the opportunity to 'switch off.' And don't just pay your subscription and waste it – turn up every time!
- Use your holiday allowance wisely and actually get away from it all. Research indicates that regular vacations reduce heart disease.
- If getting through your workload in the time available is continually too difficult for you to accomplish, then it could be that your time management is at fault. Consider signing up for a course to help you in this area.

Get that humour going

- Put some (more) humour into your environment. Liven your office up with funny quips, signs and posters. Get a humorous wall and/or desk calendar with a funny quotation for every day.

Make your presence known through laughter

As an add-on to the last bullet point, funny advertising pays off big time. Making people laugh will always put you in the forefront of your client's awareness. And their cheque book!

Laughter is the sun that drives winter from the human face.
Anonymous

So, advertise your business in a humorous way. Send amusing newsletters with funny (clean) one-liners and simple cartoons (there's usually a budding artist hiding in a cupboard, just waiting to be discovered), a humorous calendar instead of the usual run of the mill things – whatever! Just do it! Because clients are much more likely to retain and use something that amuses them – and a calendar, or coasters, that makes them laugh every day of the year is fantastic.

So, hey, guys and gals, get on and give yourself every funny, bigger and better chance you can of pulling in more business.

I digress: I'm now going back and continuing with number ...

18. Reward. Reward. Reward yourself when things go well, when things go awry and when things simply don't go at all. Just keep patting yourself on the back, concentrate only on the positives and keep your eye on the doughnut, not on the hole.

19. Don't bottle things up inside you, it's a sure fire recipe for building resentment and bitterness. Find a good listening ear and off-load whatever's buzzing around in your head. Preferably someone unconnected with your problems and, guys, I mean you too. Off-loading is not just for gals. Call it networking if it makes you feel better, so just do it and banish stress to the dungeons of your mind.

Everything begins with a thought

If you hit your thumb with a hammer, ouch, it hurts. You run cold water over it, dab in the soothing, antiseptic cream, put a plaster or a bandage round it – pop a brace or two of pills and down large measures of G & T until the soreness passes.

But ... coping with the painful feelings caused by your thoughts? Now, that can often be a great big empire-state-building problem when, no matter how hard you try to banish such thoughts to those good old dungeons ... it just doesn't happen.

So, for those times when you're really feeling knotted up inside, here's a trick that can knock those feelings into touch. This technique takes practise. Though, believe me, the more you practise you give it, the more powerful it gets.

Here's the trick

Identify where, in your body, this anxious feeling is strongest. Then notice which way it is moving (oh, yes it does, it always moves). Is the sensation going round and round? If so, which way is it turning? Clockwise or anti-clockwise? Or is it moving up and down? Or side to side? Be sure about this now, it's important.

For the purpose of explaining this technique to you, I'm going to assume that the anxious feeling is in the pit of your stomach and spinning in a clockwise direction. Now, here's what you do.

1. Sit in a comfortable position with your eyes closed.
2. Concentrate on the anxious feeling and focus on that part of your body where it feels strongest.
3. Make quite sure that you identify which way the sensation is moving.
4. Stay still and calm for a minute or so, focusing on the feeling and its location.
5. Now, keeping the movement going in the same way, mentally remove it from inside your body and place it outside your body, immediately over the inner position. The movement should be mentally visualised just a few inches from your body. (Remember, here, I'm using the example of a circle spinning clockwise. I'll give you other variations shortly).
6. Still in a relaxed sitting position, with your eyes gently closed, keep the sensation moving outside of your body.
7. Now, make this feeling spin around in the opposite direction, i.e. anti-clockwise.
8. Make it spin faster and faster, faster and faster, faster and faster.
9. Keep it spinning as fast as possible (faster, faster ...) and sing some 'clown music.' Um pum diddle iddle um pum pi dum, um pum diddle iddle um pum pi dum' (don't worry if you get your diddles, iddles, ums, pums and dums mixed up, just sing

them vigorously, really get the speed going and diddle and iddle as if your very life depends on it, like the clowns in the circus ring, frantically dashing round and round in their slapstick routine.
10. Really spin that circle around as fast as you're able (remember – opposite way to how it felt initially) – to your loud iddles, diddles, ums and pums tune.
11. Keep this movement going – faster and faster, for at least four minutes.
12. Stop singing and, keeping the movement still spinning in this 'opposite' direction, mentally put it back into its original position inside your body.
13. Keep the movement spinning (still in the opposite direction) for a couple of minutes.
14. Relax.
15. Open your eyes and notice how different you feel.
16. Has the anxious sensation lessened? Maybe it's even gone away completely.

This technique, as I said previously, needs practise. The more you do it, the better you get at it; so that, ultimately, it will be second nature to you.

Uppie downies and the rest

Maybe your sensation moves up and down, or from side to side – it may even move diagonally.

- If your feeling moves from side to side, then you change its direction to up and down.
- If your feeling moves from side to side, then you change its direction to up and down.
- If your feeling moves diagonally it will, obviously, be either down left to up right or down right to up left. Simply exchange one for the other.

On average, every year each member of staff will take sick leave, naming stress as the reason. These absences incur lost money for the company, in both wages and revenue, through reduced productivity.

The bad news

Any employee that is experiencing stress from their job, is four times more likely to suffer further damaging exhaustion, resign from their position or, ultimately, do both.

Recruitment and re-training costs for each individual can be expected to be between £3,000 and £16,000.

In addition, if an employee feels that the company has been negligent in dealing with their stress issues then litigation may result, thereby adding a greater financial burden on the company.

Now for the good news

> *'Of the British companies that introduced significant work life balance and stress management programmes, 46% said productivity had risen, while 72% thought it had fostered good employment relations.'*
>
> Employment Trends,
> Journal of General Management

This brings us back, therefore, to the fact that humour is diametrically opposite to stress. Therefore:

- if employees have fun at work, it is beneficial for both worker and company
- when people enjoy their work, it improves the bottom line
- not only does humour make the workplace more enjoyable and productive, it also creates a great environment for encouraging customers and clients to spend, spend, spend!

> '...a healthier workforce improves productivity and performance. The health and well being of people is a core issue for management. A healthy workforce is a pre-condition for competitiveness and business success ...'
>
> Our Healthier Nation
White Paper 1999

Breathing is healthy ... or not!

Breathing is a serious matter. So, I'm seriously writing about the matter of breathing.

Chronic habitual hyperventilation syndrome

I mentioned hyperventilation back on page 88. It's a subject very dear to my heart and I have around twenty year's experience helping clients recover from this unpleasant and, often, very debilitating, problem. So, if you recognise yourself in the following description folk, just give me a call.

Chronic Habitual Hyperventilation Syndrome can reduce life to a frazzle. I want to help you get back to having fun.

It's quite normal to hyperventilate when under stress. Sadly, with today's exacting lifestyle, it's common for hyperventilation to become a habit, known as Chronic Habitual Hyperventilation Syndrome (HVS). This can trigger a long, alarming list of symptoms and, at its most chronic, HVS can actually masquerade as potentially life threatening illnesses like heart disease or cancer.

Chronic HVS is an extremely insidious illness. The first attack is commonly experienced when the causing factor has actually been eliminated. For example a hard-working executive may experience the first attack at weekends or on holiday, when the stress is off. Anxiety then develops as a result of the symptoms experienced, thereby increasing the possibility of another attack. I use a hard-working executive as a typical example because type 'A' personalities are prime candidates for HVS, i.e. a workaholic, a perfectionist, or someone with an obsessional personality.

If HVS is the only problem a patient is experiencing, then a doctor may have difficulty in diagnosing it, because the symptoms can be so varied and can relate to virtually any part of the body – thyroid, cardiac, gastro-intestinal, respiratory, or central nervous system disease.

Also, if HVS is the only problem, all tests will produce a negative result. Therefore, at this stage, patients are frequently 'dismissed' as neurotic, anxious, or having hysterical fits. Regrettably, (dare I say it?) the vast majority of the medical profession do not appear to accept chronic HVS as being the debilitating illness that it is.

Symptoms can include:
Dizziness, pins and needles, numbness in lips, fingertips and toes, physical and mental depression, heart palpitations, chest pains, migraine, irritable, dry cough, chest tightness, stomach disturbances (such as indigestion, nausea, wind, or irritable bowel), muscle pains or tremors, tiredness, weakness, fainting, disturbed sleep and nightmares, phobias, clammy hands, high anxiety, excessive sighing and yawning, dislike of bright lights and loud noises, attacks of breathlessness when resting (this is usually one of the last symptoms to appear).

Hyperventilators have a tendency to cry a lot, without knowing the reason why, and there can be significant memory problems. Perhaps the most disturbing symptoms are psychic disturbances, ranging from tension through free-floating anxiety to 'unreal' feelings, called depersonalisation (when a person feels detached from what is happening around him or her) and there can be hallucinations.

The treatment to correct the faulty breathing of HVS (which can be a lengthy procedure) includes specialised relaxation techniques and focused breathing exercises to re-educate the mind and body to start breathing correctly again, from the diaphragm.

Laughs a day keep the doctor at bay
Anatomy Of An Illness, by Norman Cousins, is a book well worth reading if you want to absorb the true benefits that laughter has on your health.

In this book, Cousins tells his personal and remarkable story of how a combination of laughter and vitamin C helped him overcome the crippling, degenerative and supposedly incurable degenerative disease, ankylosing spondylitis.

After discovering, whilst in hospital, that laughter gave him some relief from his relentless, agonising pain, Cousins decided to take control of his own life, illness and the treatment of it. So, he checked himself out of hospital and into an hotel, where he could watch comedy films whenever he wanted.

With a combination of laughter and the lucky support of his doctor who helped him to start taking megadoses of vitamin C, (then, and now, against conventional wisdom), Cousin's condition began to improve.

Thus, Cousins became a pioneer in modem western society as he tapped into, and used, his own body's powers to heal itself. A couple of decades ago, the methods he used to bring about his incredible recovery would have been dismissed as hogwash. Now, in both medical and scientific fields, it's being acknowledged that our bodies are more than a collection of organs that need drugs in order to 'fix them'.

Back to the fun

I want to share my day with you, because it's been fun. It's 7pm on 7th July 2006 and, as I'm sitting at my computer writing this book, I can look out of my study window and see the beautiful Wiltshire countryside ... and my garden that looks more like an abandoned builder's yard!

And that's exactly the reason why my day has been such fun.

Let me explain.

I'm having a conservatory put on the back of my house. Actually, it's up now and there's just the decorating and, oh yes, the air conditioning/heating has to be fitted. I'm sooooo thrilled with this conservatory, folk – I'm just like a small child with a new play house because ... I'm going to use this new extension as my study – hey, it will be like sitting in the garden all day, every day, busily tapping away at the keyboard ... Okay! I tell a little white lie! ... I'll be there most days. Oh, alright then, half a day now and then.

Come on folk, have a heart, these books don't write themselves, you know, even if I am having a whale of a time doing it.

Whoops, I've just remembered. I was going to share my fun day with you.

It's been just brilliant because the three lads that put up the conservatory are now landscaping (that's a posh word for digging up the lawn; erecting and painting decking and fences; building a couple of low walls, and laying paving slabs) the garden. And these lads have so much fun whilst they're working. They see the funny side of everything and, of course, I join in. They've got used to me now and these lads no longer quake in their shoes when I tell them (with a straight face) that the concrete footings they've put in are a yard out, so they now (politely, I must hasten to add) give me as good as they get.

It's great fun having these guys around and I shall miss them big time when they leave.

Mind you, I'll get a darn sight more writing done when I don't have to constantly make important life changing decisions, like whether decking boards are better placed flat or upright, shall I brew beer in the water butt and would lights in the pond be problematic for an epileptic goldfish?

All these time consuming tasks sure do eat into the workings of a gal's fun day – and I didn't even mention the frequent, onerous task of making endless supplies of strong builder's tea, did I?

And there is a definite art to getting the tea in the mug as well as eight heaped teaspoonsful of sugar!

So, if this book is late off the press, blame three lads, umpteen flagons of flat beer and an epileptic goldfish!

By which time, I will undoubtedly be ensconced, and revelling, in the delights of my new 'garden' study – and back to my usual position in the working hierarchy, namely .....

The solitary worker

Now, I know that I just said I would miss the three lads when their smiling faces no longer appeared on my doorstep every morning, but that doesn't mean that I'm likely to drop into the depths of a deep clinical depression.

On the contrary, it means that I'll be able to work, skive, duck and dive (without interruption) in my new landscaped environment, with all the benefits of being a solitary home office worker.

Of course, there are disadvantages to working on one's own (as there are to most things). However, this situation need not necessarily be either a lonely job, or a humorously barren one.

As I hammer away at this keyboard right now (should that be write now?) I actually both live and work alone. As, no doubt, do hundreds of thousands of other folk.

Unless one has the personality of a recluse, however, in these circumstances it's vitally important to get the right work/play balance and …

Maintain contact with the big, wide world

It's a fact. (And, wow, what a challenging one.) Working from home definitely puts an entirely different slant on 'leaving for the office'.

Just stepping over the metal strip that separates your living accommodation from the working environment doesn't have quite the same feel to it as putting on your coat, picking up your car keys, going through the front door, driving to the office, arriving at, and then walking into, a totally different building.

All this stuff provides a great transition time for the brain; it gives you an opportunity to change your thought patterns; and gives structure to your day.

Without this structure, the home office worker is faced with temptation, temptation, temptation to …

… stay in bed longer; linger over breakfast; stack the dishwasher; empty the teapot; tidy the kitchen; dust and vacuum; clean the windows; sunbathe in the garden; watch television; read the newspaper; stroke the cat; play ball with the dog; clean out the gerbil;

talk to the parrot; telephone a friend and arrange to ...

... meet for lunch ...

... so, there's no point in starting work because, well, hey, you've just arranged to go out for lunch, so that makes it necessary for you to find the time to change into something smarter.

So, now you might just as well relax over another mug of coffee, before getting changed at your leisure, and set off good and early for your lunch appointment – just in case you have difficulty with parking.

All this sounding familiar? Or are you really disciplined? If so, do you recognise this scenario?

You've worked solidly for a whole week – well, almost, you've made it to Friday afternoon. That's almost five days in total isolation. You've written letters, reports and, maybe an article or two; got the filing up to date and sent out all your invoices; done some incredibly deep research – so you've achieved a lot and you're feeling really good about that.

However, the pressure is now really getting to you – not from work – from sheer isolation and loneliness.

Hardly surprising eh? After all, this is your fifth day totally devoid of any meaningful communication with the big, wide world out there. Or, now you come to think about it, could it even be the sixth or seventh day?

You panic now. Maybe it's Saturday today, or even Sunday. Have you actually missed the weekend altogether?

It's Monday??? !!!

Frantically you check your diary (and your mobile phone, to do a belt and braces job) to confirm that ... thank goodness, it is Friday, of this week.

The sense of relief, however, is short lived as the feeling of isolation kicks in again and it just seems to saturate your whole body.

Has planet earth drifted from its axis and floated off into space? you wonder, peering out of the window, half expecting the toothless grin of an alien to stare back at you, a UFO to fly by, or a lost astronaut to enquire if he can borrow your copy of 'The Hitchhikers Guide To The Galaxy.'

Now, home workers, you don't need me to tell you that, when you've reached this point, you have completely, utterly, without doubt, and totally unaided by human being, telephone or budgerigar, lost the plot.

You've reached one of those momentous points that all home workers must learn to recognise in order to instigate rapid changes to prevent this empty feeling in the pit of your stomach rapidly deteriorating to the depths of irreversible, manic, insanity.

Are you keeping up with me here?

Time for an important mental health check

Do you:
- feel as if you're in a forgotten void; ensnared in a chasm where, even if you had died, it's unlikely that anybody would notice, let alone advise your dear old Aunty Ethel?
- read and re-read your emails and faxes for comfort and to remind yourself that somebody, from time to time, actually thinks about you?
- save telephone messages and replay them just to hear another human voice?
- constantly check the telephone lines to make sure they're still connected and fully operational?
- find yourself frequently looking down the road through your binoculars hoping to find a cat, dog, or escaped hampster that you could coax in with a bowl of milk to discuss the trials and tribulations of re-cycling waste paper, the vagaries of printer ink cartridges and whether pot noodle soup is the greatest invention of all time?
- regularly decide that your binoculars are not powerful enough and need to buy a very large telescope that you could permanently site in a strategic position on the roof?
- seriously consider calling the Samaritans and feigning loss of memory, in the hope that a sympathetic volunteer will call round in person with buckets of tender, loving care? Better still, oodles

of chocolate to pump up your blood sugar content and ensure that your cholesterol levels don't feel abandoned?
- attempt to drum up courage to join Alcoholics Anonymous, just so that you can attend their weekly meetings, meet people and have a few intoxicating conversations?

Results

If you answered yes to one or more of the above questions, then it's absolutely imperative that you take immediate action to prevent the onset of chronic, progressive, degenerative, home worker's psychosis.

If you answered no, don't take any chances. Remember the adage 'prevention is better than cure' and take every precaution to ensure the continuance of your good mental health and general well being because ...

... without doubt, one of the home worker's biggest challenges is maintaining social contact with the big wide world – and bringing real humour into the one man (whoops, one-person) workplace.

Cyber contact is simply not sufficient – this barely touches the periphery of the isolation.

So, hey come on, folk, snap out of it.

It's get up, go, get down and have some fun time!

Eliminate the negative: accentuate the positive: don't mess with mister in-between

Although you may find that working alone proves to be one of your most challenging experiences, when approached in the right manner, it can certainly provide you with opportunities to also experience some incredibly rewarding times.

So, if you're a member of the work from home brigade, I urge you to stop pampering, right now, to the daily grind and begin to incorporate huge dollops of humour into it.

Am I crazy? Am I serious?

Yes, you're darn right I am. On both counts. I'm just crazy about seriously introducing humour and laughter into your workplace. And making fun work!

So, solitary home workers, I urge you, (yet again), to make humour an integral, important part of your working life.

Remember, having fun is a tremendous company asset. It's far more valuable than computers, photocopiers or telephones – it's even more valuable than the coffee machine!

Why? Why is laughter more valuable than any other piece of office equipment?

Here's why:

- Because equipment is only as effective as the person that operates it; and so, if you're a solo office worker, the level of success of your organisation is entirely dependent upon the state of mind of ... you!

  Again, I reiterate what I've said earlier, humour is not about telling jokes, being funny, or generally acting the clown.
- Humour is all about noticing the absurdity in the illogical, irrational things that life throws at us; and using those absurdities and illogicalities (Does such a word exist? It does now!) to turn a potentially stressful problem into a creative opportunity.

  What I'm saying, in brief, is that a good sense of humour helps you achieve, and maintain, a healthy, balanced outlook on your work and life.
- Humour enables you to make light of serious work. And, as a solo home worker (in the wonderful, enviable, position of being a 'committee of one') you decide to take full advantage of the numerous ways in which you can combine humour with business.

  Read on ... for serious suggestions to make your work easy; boost your motivation and creativity, de-press your di-stress and increase the pleasure (that feeling of hey yes wow pow zing zang every time you step into your home office).

Make your environment fun

Consider this:

- Do you feel happier on a sunny day than you do on a rainy one?
- Do you feel better when you're comfortable or uncomfortable?
- Does a bright colour lift your spirits more than a dark one?
- Are your spirits lifted more by laughter than depression?
- Will a brighter environment lift your mood or lower it?

When all kinds of folk have been asked these questions, in all kinds of places and situations, the answers have shown that we are greatly affected by our environment. Therefore, if your work place presents a tired and glum image, with depressing paintwork, shabby this and that in a room that generally induces an overwhelming sense of calamitous anonymity, sending your soul spiralling into a deep ravine of despondency and 'heck, what's it all about?' ...

... Wake up!

Are you, or are you not, the person who makes all the decisions around the place?

Readers, and home office colleagues, just remind yourself of your exalted position now. You are the Chairman ... whoops, done it again ... I mean, chairperson, secretary, treasurer and sole member of the company that you own!

But, hey, does it matter what you call yourself when you are Chief Executive Of Everything, Manager Of Each Division and Head of Every Department?

So, now's the time to score solo big time over the guys in the great big empire-state-building corporate world. You can paint the walls of your workplace any colour you want – no necessity to settle here for faithful magnolia, migraine mustard or peach haze with deep purple ripples just because Works and Services Department bought a job lot of paint that would cover the entire city of London plus the outskirts of Skegness and the walls of every cell in Dartmoor prison!

Go **mad**. Go **wild**. Go **liven, brighten** and **cheer up** your work place in your favourite, brilliant colours. (Okay, so you like peach haze with deep purple ripples – whatever makes you feel good).

Take a close look at the blinds, curtains – or both.

Are they crying out for a trip to the dry cleaners, need shortening, lengthening or, hey, be honest now that you've taken a very long, hard look at them, should you actually replace the lot?

What about the floor now? Have the carpet or tiles seen better days? How about investing in a modern, stylish wooden floor?

When you've sorted out the walls, windows and floor it's time to display those funny posters, pictures, photographs, cartoons, quotations (a large bulletin board is useful for these smaller things).

Does having some music playing in the background help you work better? Then it's time to extend the cabling on your stereo system and put a couple of dinky speakers on your office wall.

Granted, we all have our different tastes in music, though I suggest you try playing some inspirational music first thing in the morning to get you fired up for the fray! Day! Whatever!

Have a few toys around the place – some of those relaxing things that work miracles in unwinding the mind and releasing creativity.

When clients visit

Clients are usually really happy to join in with the fun. Encourage it and, ten to one, they'll start sending you emails with funny quotations and stories, jokes, and humorous snippets. This is a great way to maintain good client liaison.

However, if you have a new client coming to your home office, one that you're unsure about or, indeed, anyone who may not yet be a registered member of your elite humour brigade here's ...

Plan B

Stick a Monet or a Constable print on the back of your bulletin board; put diplomas or receipts for your subscriptions to favourite charities on the back of pictures and remember to turn every frame over before your client arrives.

Put all other 'questionable' smaller items in a cupboard or drawer and replace these with sedate family photographs. That is, if you wish to portray yourself as a committed, loyal family person.

The alternative? Well, just how do you wish to portray yourself when you want this client to both respect you and give you thousands of pounds worth of repeat business? Hmmm?

Switch off the music or play something appropriate in the background. Sticking with the inspirational music is usually a good strategy.

Do you remember Bill Haley?

For those of you who don't remember Bill Haley, the rock'n'roll icon, and to jog the memory of those that do, Bill Haley recorded *Rock Around The Clock*.

And, readers, this is exactly what I want you to start doing – rocking around the clock, that is.

Because many, if not all, of you home workers have undoubtedly found yourself in the position of working around the clock – at some time or other. Maybe you're still doing it and are now marooned on an island of dreariness, where life seems all work, no play and fun seems a dim and distant memory.

Take a break

Working around the clock is bad news for your stress buds – or good news – depending upon which road you're travelling.

Are you travelling down Your Road, which takes you along a contented, meaningful, productive pathway and is, therefore, the Right Road? Or are you ambling down the less productive Stress Road, dipping in and out of potholes of discontent, reduced productivity and unfulfillment? Clearly, the Wrong Road.

It's decision time, my friends

How about deciding that, from this moment on, you will constantly, and wholeheartedly, travel down Your Road; never letting yourself be tempted to allow your stress buds to get so much as a glimpse of the light of day. Remember, if you do, they are sure to reproduce faster than ... well, let me just say that the speed at which rabbits reproduce is minuscule, compared with the reproductive cycle of stress. Given half a chance, a bud becomes a cotton pickin' plantation. So ...

Take another break
Working non-stop, refusing to give in to a feeling of weariness and pushing yourself through the tiredness barrier, is oh so counter-productive. Although we now live in a highly scientific, technical, aeronautical world of space rockets, computers and coconut smoothies, your mind and body still basically operate in prehistoric, cave man mode.

Your physiology is just not built for working endless hours without a break. And centuries of evolution, and all the changes and progress that have been made through these hundreds and thousands of years, have not altered your ability, or adjusted your coping mechanism, to deal any more successfully with the stress that is caused through constant over work.

Your mind and body will, sooner or later, still object to it – just as it would have done centuries ago.

Did the caveman hunt after dark? Or struggle to do things in the dim light of his fire? No. He went to sleep and his tasks would be left until the next light of day.

So, my friends, don't tempt fate. Decide what your 'working hours' will be within your 'working week' and then schedule some playful, relaxing, humour breaks into your days.

Just remember that useful word 'organisation', and that important phrase 'time management'.

Create your plan of campaign. Stick to it like a military manoeuvre. And you will reap the benefit.

The results will be incredible. You will find yourself more alert, more creative and more productive.

You're in prime position
The solo home worker is in a far better position than any employee to schedule, and take, frequent breaks. Those important times that, research indicates, enable you to manage stress much better. Indeed, you could even find that you have eliminated those stressful feelings altogether by scheduling regular time out for relaxation.

Relaxation and fun should be an integral part of your day, not a possibility at the end of it

Occupational Chuckles

- I used to be a doctor, but I ran out of patients.
- I used to be a dentist, but it was only a filler job.
- I used to be a lavatory technician, but my career went down the pan.
- I used to be a pilot, but my career didn't take off.
- I used to be a fighter pilot, but my dreams were shot down.
- I used to be a fireman, but my dreams went up in smoke.
- I used to be a sailor, but my career sank.
- I used to be an architect, but I couldn't build up my career.
- I used to make doors, but I couldn't get a handle on it.
- I used to be a hairdresser, but I got cut short.
- I used to be a gardener, but I was turfed out.
- I used to be a firework maker but the work just fizzled out.
- I used to be a lawn specialist but someone grassed me up.
- I used to be a locksmith but I was too keyed up.

To continue … just for the fun of it

It's a good idea to decide in advance when you will take your humour breaks, how long they will be and what you intend to do with them.

I have a colleague who, during the lovely summer days, pops outside and hits a few croquet balls around the lawn. Another one practises his golf.

During the colder, winter months, you might decide to amuse yourself by singing silly music hall songs and accompanying yourself on the piano; strumming a guitar, learning to play the saxophone or trumpet, or even mastering the bagpipes.

How about watching a bit of comedy on the television, reading a chapter of your current book, tickling your cat's tummy or giving your dog ten minutes exercise?

I read somewhere that Thomas Edison took time out to play with his dog – and what a fine role model he was. Thomas Edison, that is, not the dog.

Oh, I dunno. Could be the dog. It did appear to give Edison inspiration.

And opposite are some inspiration from the Church.

You can chuckle over these parish announcements all on your own.

Churchy Chuckles

- Pot luck supper. Sunday at 5pm. Prayer and medication to follow.

- The Fasting and Prayer Conference includes meals.

- The sermon this morning is 'Jesus walks on the water.' The sermon this evening is 'Searching for Jesus.'

- Next week there will be trials for the choir; they need all the help they can get.

- A bean supper will be held on Tuesday evening in the Church Hall; music will follow.

- The topic for the sermon this evening is 'What is hell?' Come early and listen to our choir practice.

- Eight new choir robes are currently needed due to the addition of several new members and the deterioration of some older ones.

- This evening, at 7pm, there will be hymn singing in the park across from the church. Bring a blanket and come prepared to sin.

- The primary 7's will be presenting Shakespeare's 'Hamlet' in the Church basement. From 7pm, the congregation is invited to attend this tragedy.

- The Church will host an evening of fine dancing, superb entertainment and gracious hostility.

And more for the solitary worker

Boys' and girls' toys
Keep a ready supply of 'humour cues' in your work place. Books of funny quotations, jokes, or humorous cartoons, childish toys and games – any silly thing that will make you laugh like a four year-old.

Loudly and without restraint.

Whatever you decide to do, be disciplined about it. Stick to the time that you've allotted yourself and don't ever be tempted to have 'just a few minutes more.'

Oh, by the way, let the answerphone take calls during your break. Be strict about the work/fun divide.

Talking about telephones has, for some reason known only to my sub-conscious, made me think about the number of people who seem to be totally incapable of driving a car without talking to someone on their mobile as they drive.

It's almost as if these folk think the phone will forget how to work if they don't use it all the time they're behind the driving wheel.

The times I've seen someone clamber into their vehicle, slam the door shut and start keying a number into their cell phone ... I wonder ... just how many life or death situations is it possible for one person to have in one day?

Ah, but you're not one of those people are you? (Are you?) And you don't act like that, do you? (Do you?)

Nooooo. You're a calm, dignified, organised home worker. A person that has relinquished all necessity for a car to get you to and from work each day; you're no longer a member of the mobile basket case brigade, because you no longer have to endure the daily office commute.

What bliss!

Now, every day, in every way, you can delight in …..

The joys of non-commuting

Joy upon joy for the home worker. No need to leave home at some unearthly hour to beat the early morning traffic and no more staying late at the office to miss the evening rush hour.

Just how much pleasure can you stand?

Particularly on those days when you peep out of your bedroom window and see the snow piled high against your garage door and the most energetic thing you have to do is utter phew and aha and listen to the weather forecast to find out when a thaw is expected.

However, unless you're extremely lucky, chances are high that work will necessitate your having to brave the roads and travel sometime, somewhere, to see somebody.

Now, you might be one of those folk who prefer to do just about anything but get behind the wheel of a car; or you may be like me and get a buzz from exchanging your isolated, static home office for an (let's face it) equally isolated, mobile one.

Yippee! I can conjure up that buzzy feeling right now – just by thinking about it!

So, this makes it time to give myself a humour break.

Mmm! I rather fancy an ice cream! One of those white chocolate things!

Back to travel and feeling good

Wherever thou shalt venture, the quirks and perils of driving – road works, diversions, breakdowns, bad weather, and traffic jams (not to mention coping with those ass-like drivers who prefer your lane of traffic to theirs – and nonchalantly move into it without so much as a by your leave) are planning to incite a civil war between your body and mind.

Therefore, great care must be taken to prevent these highway plotters hastening your entry into the dimly lit corridors of the local psychiatric hospital. Unless, that is, your 'vacation kitty' is in the red or the VAT inspector is hot on your trail and the local psychi seems preferable to the local cell.

The road that cheers

For the purpose of this book, I shall keep things simple and assume that you've decided (a) sanity is the best policy and (b) the VAT inspector believes denial is just a river in Egypt.

I therefore offer you some common-sensical suggestions for maintaining your humorous demeanour throughout every perilous sojourn on the high-ways, low-ways and all-other-road-ways.

Your vehicle
This is your mobile office and its appearance says a lot about you. So clean (or, preferably, have someone do it for you) your car regularly, both inside and out. And keep it neat and tidy.

It's surprising how much better you'll feel driving a well-groomed vehicle.

Car phone
I've already touched (heavily) on this subject. Unless your call is really urgent, let it wait. This is your time, so guard it zealously and use it wisely.

Relax, listen and laugh
Do avoid the temptation to turn on the car radio and listen to which country has been invaded, who's been shot and what foods are bad for you. You need to arrive at your appointments in a buoyant mood and focused on your own well being; not feeling as if you're doing the job of every member of the British Government.

Take full advantage of this opportunity to pop your favourite tunes into the car's music box; laugh along with recordings of your favourite sitcoms, have a giggle at one of those recorded, humorous books or enjoy chuckling at CDs of stand-up comedians

Anyway, anyhow, whatever
The above are some suggestions. Use them, lose them, add to them ... whatever suits you. It's your choice ... to just do something to make you laugh!

Play is for anyone, of any age
Just because you grew up, left school and now have to make some money to pay your own bills, it doesn't mean that you have to abandon your childhood completely. (Yep, I'm on about childhood again!)

Hey, you didn't discard your body just because you grew up. Did you? Leastways, not voluntarily. That change of shape was just – well – kind of coincidental!

So, what made most of you let go of that playful bit? (Yep, that's the one – the bit you let go when you were told to 'grow up'.) Well, I want you to go right back and get a hold of that playful bit and bring it right slap bang up to date.

And I want you to hold on to that playfulness forever, so that you, and everyone else, can enjoy yourselves right now. And even then!

In the corporate world

For those of you that work in one of those places where there are other folk, I'm going to give you some crazy ideas for making work together fun work.

Before you shake your head in disbelief and say 'That's just downright stupid' remember – that's the whole point!

You must get really serious about this fun business.

First, a bit of info
Research has indicated that gerbils, when kept in barren, dull, box-like compartments actually lose their brain cells. Whereas those that were kept in a colourful environment, with stimulating toys around them, actually grew more brain cells.

Mmm. So, might our environment affect us mere mortals in a similar way? Food for thought eh?

Anyhow, take a look at my suggestions; expand on them; and use these ideas as a starting handle to crank your own engines.

Here come the crazies

Comedy picnic lunch:	Watch a comedy video over the lunch break and everyone can eat their lunch while they're watching it. (That is, if they can eat and laugh at they same time.)
Favourite music day:	Take a vote on your favourite group or singer and play their music for the whole day.

Impersonation contest:	Either choose to have one personality for everyone to impersonate or let it be free choice.
Public celebration days:	Check out when other countries have special days and celebrate them yourself. With just a tiny amount of luck, you should be able to have a celebration most days.
Look-alike contest:	Have an Ali G look-alike competition (or a Frank Spencer one if you're a bit older in the tooth).
Tennis match:	Organise a mixed doubles tennis match or a badminton game.
Slippers day:	Have a 'wear slippers to work' day.
Treasure hunt:	Organise a car treasure hunt or even have one in the office.
Spoil someone day:	Put corresponding numbers in a hat and the people who draw the same numbers have to buy each other a cream cake, bar of chocolate, or whatever.
Bosses exchange day:	Have the bosses make coffee and tea and take the mail to the post office.
Sitcom break:	Show sitcom videos during the lunch break.
Wild west day:	Everyone dresses up in wild west attire.
April fool's day:	Have a May Fool's Day; or a July one: in fact as many as you like, but remember they all have to end by midday.
Shipwreck:	Turn up for the office in what you were wearing when 'the ship went down'.

Charades:	Schedule ten-minute breaks for a game of charades.
Talent contest:	Everyone must do a two minute spot.
Skittles contest:	Organise the workforce into teams and have an evening at the skittle alley. You may have to invite partners, friends and family along to boost the numbers.
Match the baby competition:	Everyone provides a photograph of themselves as a baby and people have to guess who it is.
Quiz night:	Organise a quiz night at your local. This is another event where you might have to invite 'extras' along to swell the ranks. Most pubs are willing to let you have a room for free in return for the drinks they sell. If you ask them to provide supper as well, so much the better.
Radio comedy:	Play CDs of stand up comics.
Silly hat day:	Give a prize for the silliest hat.
Prime Minister competition:	Name as many Prime Ministers as possible. Give additional points for knowing their years in office.
US President Competition:	Same as above.
Race day:	Organise a day at the races.
Name that animal:	Put up pictures of wild animals for everyone to identify. Give the winner a family ticket to the zoo.
Spot the SMS:	Everyone sends a secret SMS to a colleague and the recipient must guess who

	sent it. The winner gets a £5 mobile phone voucher.
Theatre trips:	Create a theatre club and organise regular visits.
Croquet:	If you're lucky enough to have some grass outside your work place, put up the croquet hoops and enjoy the fresh air. Create a summer league to provide some friendly competition.
Social evenings:	Organise monthly 'no work talk' social evenings. Definitely no 'housekeeping' notices allowed and anyone who mentions work will have to pay a funny forfeit.
Humour board:	The biggest you can find or, better still, many smaller ones dotted around the place. Encourage everyone to post cartoon strips, jokes, funny articles from newspapers, magazines, etc. Anything that's fun, but please insist that it's good clean fun.
Funny logo:	Have a competition for the funniest departmental logo.
Silly days:	Organise a silly sunhat, or a comical dress day
Halloween:	Don't let the children have all the fun. Organise your own.
Pet peeve:	This is the time when everyone gets an opportunity to air their minor work irritations. Even the simplest peeve must be seriously addressed by everyone to prevent it happening in future.

Birthdays:	Don't just stick to the 'cream cake' routine. Make everyone's birthday a really special time.
Declaration day:	Have a Declaration Day for anything you like. Just name your topic, decide the day and declare it!
Inventor's Day:	Find out when things were invented, radio, television, microwave, for example and celebrate it.
Barbecue:	Hold a barbecue to celebrate the first day of summer.
Pie and Chips:	Have a pie and chips evening to celebrate the last day of winter.

Something, anything and more – to remind everyone not to take themselves too seriously

Beware of the culture vulture

Research carried out by Peter Fleming of the University of Cambridge, revealed that many companies encountered a lot of cynicism when they attempted to introduce the fun culture into their organisation.

Peter's Fleming's findings revealed that employees were very doubtful about their employer's motives and suspected a hidden agenda, i.e. to increase profits rather than to increase employee satisfaction.

Humour is not a sticking plaster

Clearly, therefore, very great care must be taken to ensure that humour is used to truly *enhance* your organisation. Any attempt to use humour as a *sticking plaster to cover cracks* will only result in the plaster coming unstuck and revealing the bare and imperfect bones of your organisation!

Humour is not what you do – it's what you are.

Humour is not about doing – it's about being.

Humour is neither a beginning, nor an end, in itself. It's a tool that can turn dreariness into fun, sorrow into happiness, and a job into a passion.

Within the working world, humour and fun are valuable assets that nestle within the very heart of a healthy, respectful, inspired and motivated workforce.

And what about those important customers?

I have favourite places (as, I expect, do you) where I shop, for both goods and services. These are mostly within easy reach of my home. However, in the case of my hairdresser, I make a one hundred and twenty mile round trip for the pleasure and privilege of receiving their excellent customer care.

And to have fun!

Before I moved to my present home in Wiltshire, I lived in Hampshire. My journey, then, took anything from two to four hours, depending on the traffic.

'What ... ?' do I hear you cry in horror and amazement? *'What's so special about this hairdressing salon that Annie will regularly, willingly and very eagerly, make this journey?'*

I'll explain

Firstly, let me remind you of the quotation on page 6 of this book. These are the words of Darrell Blake, co-owner and Managing Director of Blushes, the hairdressing salon that it is my delight, and honour, to visit.

> *Enjoy what you do*
> *and*
> *you will never work a day in your life.*

Blushes hairdressing salons (in Cheltenham and Gloucester) are the epitome of excellence, for both employees and clients.

Owned by brothers Darrell and Mark Blake, Blushes offers customer service that is second to none, and a working environment in which every member of staff exudes passion.

Here, in rural Gloucestershire, clients are treated to hairstyles, cutting and colouring techniques that can normally only be found in top London salons. Blushes is right up there at the pinnacle of the hairdressing industry, with members of its large band of skilled stylists winning top team and individual awards. Employee's creative hair designs can be found on the front cover of leading magazines such as *Tatler* and *Vogue*.

Most definitely, Blushes is a huge success.

And there's more – Blushes' success is not limited to the catwalk. Its award-winning workforce is not driven by money, fame or glory. Although, naturally, these are appreciated and enjoyed, they are not at the top of the agenda.

So what is?

Passion

Everyone at Blushes is passionate about their work and they make every client feel special.

Whenever I walk into this light, spacious and well-equipped salon, I am treated like a queen. A friendly receptionist greets me with a smile, my coat is taken and placed neatly on a hanger and I never have a lengthy wait before … I am indulged with the highest standards of organisation, service, customer care and top know-how … in an atmosphere of fun!

This organisation is built on passion, teamwork, consideration, and enjoyment. Staff are recruited as much for their personality as for their ability.

Take note all ye others

I offer Blushes as an outstanding example of everything that I have been encouraging in this book. And other companies would do well to follow the principles and examples of this excellently run, fun organisation.

Weekly staff meetings are held to keep everyone up to date with the management's plans and ideas; to hear and discuss employees' thoughts; and to air and sort out any concerns.

Teamwork is the name of the game at Blushes and the result is electrifying.

Motivation leads to better teamwork

Better teamwork means a happier organisation

A happier organisation has lower turnover of staff

Lower turnover of staff promotes self worth

Self worth encourages reliability and stability

Stability is a sound basis for team work

Teamwork is improved through laughing together

Laughter is humour in motion

Legal Chuckles

These are some questions that attorneys actually put to witnesses during court trials. They were reported in the Massachusetts Bar Association Lawyers Journal with, in some cases, a few rather insightful replies!

- Now doctor, isn't it true that, when a person dies in his sleep, he doesn't know about it until the next morning?

- The youngest son, the twenty-year old, how old is he?

- Q: She had three children, right?
  A: Yes
  Q: How many were boys?
  A: None
  Q: How many were girls?

- Was it you, or your younger brother, who was killed in the war?

- Were you present when your picture was taken?

- Q: You say the stairs went down to the basement?
  A: Yes
  Q: And did they go up also?

- Were you alone, or by yourself?

- Q: How was your first marriage terminated?
  A: By death
  Q: And by whose death was it terminated?

- Did he kill you?

- How far apart were the vehicles at the time of the collision?

- Q: Can you describe the individual?
  A: He was about medium height and had a beard
  Q: Was this a male, or a female?

- You were there until the time you left, is that true?

- Q: Doctor, before you performed the autopsy, did you check for a pulse?
  A: No.
  Q: Did you check for blood pressure?
  A: No.
  Q: Did you check for breathing?
  A: No.
  Q: So, then it is possible that the patient was alive when you began the autopsy?
  A: No.
  Q: How can you be so sure Doctor?
  A: Because his brain was sitting on my desk in a jar.
  Q: But could the patient have still been alive nevertheless?
  A: It is possible that he could have been alive and practicing law somewhere.

Humour is an affirmation of dignity, a declaration of man's superiority to all that befalls him.
Romain Gary (1914-1980)
French Writer

Sense of humour survey

I recently carried out a survey on **The Importance of Humour in the Workplace** and I have just enough space left to give you the results.

SURVEY : BENEFITS OF HUMOUR IN THE WORKPLACE

In this survey, I asked employees whether they believed a sense of humour in the workplace was beneficial. The survey revealed that 97% of people believe that staff with a sense of humour do better at their jobs. The other 3 percent took on a glazed expression, shuffled their feet and said they would seriously consider the question.

Anyway, here are the full results of that survey:

- **Do staff with a sense of humour concentrate on their work more efficiently?**
    - 70% said yes
    - 20% said no
    - 10% asked me to repeat the question

- **Are people with a sense of humour less likely to be absent from work?**
    - 90% said yes
    - 6% said no
    - 4% couldn't answer because they were at the doctors'.

- **Are staff with a sense of humour better at tackling numerical problems?**
    - 80% said yes
    - 45% said no

- **I asked some IT people if they thought having a sense of humour helped them with their work. They said:**
    - Go to file; save as; right click, control-alt-F9; backspace; delete.

  Which was very useful. Thank you for that.

- **I asked the HR Department if they thought having a sense of humour helped them with their work.**
    - They gave me a feedback form to fill in, asking me if I felt having a sense of humour helped me with my work.

- **I asked the Finance Department. Would a sense of humour be beneficial?**
    - They said they would prepare a cost benefit analysis and let me know.

Finally, I talked with marketing
- They'll get back to me in twelve weeks.

Always laugh when you can. It's cheap medicine.
                Lord Byron (1788-1824) English Poet

Text message just received from my daughter

Don't panic, but I'm in hospital. I poisoned myself. I ate what I thought was an onion ... it was a daffodil bulb ... Doctors say I'll be out in the Spring.

Not a Conclusion

My sincere thanks to you all for reading this book, especially those who managed to get to the end without taking a nap.